Pages of Faith

Pages of Faith

The Art of Spiritual Scrapbooking

SHARON SHERIDAN

MOREHOUSE PUBLISHING

An imprint of Church Publishing Incorporated

HARRISBURG — NEW YORK

Unless otherwise noted, the Scripture quotations contained herein are from the New Revised Standard Version Bible, copyright © 1989 by the Division of Christian Education of the National Council of Churches of Christ in the U.S.A. Used by permission. All rights reserved.

The hymn texts quoted in this book are taken from *The Hymnal 1982* © 1985 by The Church Pension Fund. Used by permission.

Excerpt from The Rev. Elizabeth Kaeton's essay on The Season of Epiphanies used by permission. "Life Blessing" by Ann Prentice, OSH, used by permission.

Morehouse Publishing, 4775 Linglestown Road, Harrisburg, PA 17105
Morehouse Publishing, 445 Fifth Avenue, New York, NY 10016
Morehouse Publishing is an imprint of Church Publishing Incorporated.

Cover design by Brenda Klinger
Interior design by Beth Oberholtzer
Color insert pages redesigned by Sue Banker

Citations for 8-page color insert: Page 1 contributed and originally designed by Dawn Dowdy. Pages 2, 5, 6, and 7 contributed and originally designed by The Rev. Anne Fraley. Page 3 contributed and originally designed by Shannon Jergenson. Page 8 contributed by Judy A. Carter and originally designed by Mary Rohe.

Library of Congress Cataloging-in-Publication Data

Sheridan, Sharon.
    Pages of faith : the art of spiritual scrapbooking / Sharon Sheridan.
      p.   cm.
    Includes bibliographical references.
    ISBN 978-0-8192-2224-4 (hardcover)
    1. Storytelling—Religious aspects—Christianity. 2. Scrapbook journaling. 3. Christian life—Anecdotes. I. Title.
BT83.78.S54   2007
248.4'6—dc22
                             2007005332

Printed in the United States of America

07 08 09 10 11 12   10 9 8 7 6 5 4 3 2 1

For Carl, our Golden Dragon baby
and my favorite scrapbook subject.

CONTENTS

BUILDING COMMUNITY

BUILDING BLOCKS

ACKNOWLEDGMENTS

One of the charming things about praying with my six-year-old is that he tends to have more "thank yous" than what he calls "please prayers." I'd like to follow his model in acknowledging some of the many people who helped make this book possible.

I especially wish to thank all of the scrappers, Creative Memories consultants and industry experts who shared their ideas, resources, experience and album pages with me, including Angel Ackerman, Rhonda Anderson, Debby Ball, Lisa Bearnson, Judy Carter, Marielen Christensen, Dawn Dowdy, Terry Ferguson, Darcy Fesmire, Anne Fraley, Maurica French, Mary Hockenberry, Shannon Jergenson, Sandra Joseph, Patrice Kealy, Anne Lemay, Katherine McGlynn, Robin Montgomery, Annie Muscarella, Matt O'Keeffe, Beverly Pfau, Anna Notation-Rhoades, Mary Rohe, Suzanne Ross, Elin Siegfried, Becky Suydan and Sandy Schwalb. Thank you to Tracy Bridges, who introduced me to scrapbooking and provided invaluable advice and contacts, and to the Episcopal Communicators for spreading the word about my search for faith scrappers.

Thanks to Adrian Cross for describing the scrapbooks in the archives at St. Paul's Cathedral in Buffalo, New York, and to Mary Wieland for sharing the story of the journal she created after her son died. Thank you to Susan Tucker for her timeline and information on scrapbooking's history, to Dr. Brent Plate for his insights into the church-scrapbooking connection and to Dr. Laura Vance for increasing my knowledge of the Church of Jesus Christ of Latter-day Saints and its relation to scrapbooking. Thanks also to Jodi Hirsch and Pat Hope, who helped me understand the Rite of Christian Initiation for Adults, to Cheryl Bauman and Tonya DeLisa, who explained how scrapbooks can help babies find adoptive families at Crisis Pregnancy Outreach in Oklahoma, and to Stacy Leistner of the American National Standards Institute for unraveling the mysteries of national and international standards for archival materials.

I could not have completed this project without the moral support and technical assistance of my husband, Paul, a nonscrapper who nonetheless has a great eye and helpful suggestions for page layouts. I'm grateful to my manuscript readers—Anne Agostin, Susan Fichtelberg, Carole Ann King, Karen Siegel and Amy Tolbert—for their enthusiasm and astute but gentle critiques. Thank you also to Melissa Hartley, Elizabeth Kaeton and Ann Prentice, Order of Saint Helena, for their contributions and liturgical assistance. Thanks to Sue Stone for her sound contract advice and to Alena Langan, Maren Larsen and Maryann Rulapaugh for suggesting the book's title. And a big thanks to my editor, Nancy Fitzgerald, for shepherding me through this project and to Frank Buhrman for putting us together in the first place.

Happy scrapping!

CHAPTER 1

A PLACE TO TELL OUR STORIES

Tell your children of it,
and let your children tell their children,
and their children another generation.

—JOEL 1:3

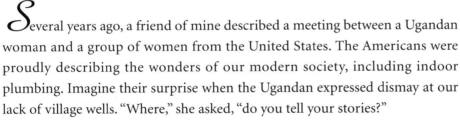

*S*everal years ago, a friend of mine described a meeting between a Ugandan woman and a group of women from the United States. The Americans were proudly describing the wonders of our modern society, including indoor plumbing. Imagine their surprise when the Ugandan expressed dismay at our lack of village wells. "Where," she asked, "do you tell your stories?"

A few months later, I reported back to my friend that I had discovered where growing numbers of American women—and some men—tell their stories. I had discovered scrapbooking.

I've always been a storyteller, and a story-gatherer. I've been accused of never answering a question with a plain "yes" or "no." But why give a simple answer when you can provide context and character? I love listening to stories, fact or fiction, folktale or family history. As a journalist, I enjoy hearing people's stories and then retelling them for a wider audience.

Scrapbooking, I have learned, is another powerful storytelling medium. First, scrapbook albums record personal and family stories, preserving that history for future generations. Scrapbooking lets you organize your thoughts as well as your photos and record names and dates and feelings that otherwise blur with time. "Scrapper" Robin Montgomery demonstrates how important this is when she recalls how her grandmother died from Alzheimer's disease, her stories and memories fading with her life. Robin herself was an only child, and her mother didn't document much family history. Robin vowed that when she married and had children, she would document everything, recording their lives, their values and their faith.

"I wanted my girls to know the stories," says the mother of two, who has created numerous family scrapbook albums. She also became a scrapbook consultant in New Jersey, helping others learn how to preserve their precious family stories.

Second, scrapbooking is a communal activity. While scrappers can, and do, work alone, they also gather regularly at workshops and "crops" to work on their albums. There, they share stories about their lives and families—not unlike the conversations around those Ugandan wells. Cropping photos around a dining room table, I've heard stories of joy and pain, recreation and reconciliation, birth and death.

Scrapbooking provides time for reflection, individually and communally. And that includes an opportunity for spiritual reflection. For me, this took the form of a baby book exploring the spirituality of my pregnancy and early days with my son. Although I had included church events in our general family scrapbook, I wanted to create an album that more deliberately traced my spiritual journey into motherhood.

I didn't get pregnant easily. Month followed disappointing month. Finally, at the dawn of 2000, I left for my annual writer's workshop and retreat with author Madeleine L'Engle at an Episcopal monastery in upstate New York. These always were particularly holy times for me. For weeks, I'd anticipate reconnecting with close friends I had met through the workshops and saw only at these events. Peace would enfold me the moment I stepped from the car onto the monastery grounds. And through the days of laughter and silence and music and writing and storytelling and prayer, I would recharge my creative and spiritual batteries.

I remember lighting a candle in the chapel that year, praying as I knelt on the hard stone floor and feeling a sense of acceptance: What would be would be. Somehow, I turned over my reproductive worries to God and moved restfully into the rhythm of the monastery and the week's events. That January, those events included sledding down a giant hill toward the Hudson River following a snowstorm. Over and over, some of the other retreatants and I hurled ourselves down the frozen hillside—on pieces of cardboard, on cafeteria trays and finally on sleds one of the brothers hauled out of the attic. After about two days of this, I realized I might, finally, be pregnant. Panicked, I sought out a fellow writer who coincidentally also was a doctor. She reassured me. Maybe, she said, all that sledding just shook everything into place.

The day after the retreat, I had a positive pregnancy test.

As usual, I had photographed the week's activities prolifically, even convincing a friend to record my descent down the snowy hill. For years, those pictures sat in an ordinary photo album, labeled only in my imagination. With my spiritual baby scrapbook, however, I could continue to save those photos along with the stories behind them. Scrappers write, or "journal," as well as mount photos in their albums; here was my chance to record those retreat memories—my prayerful surrender, the holy friendships, my panic and then my joyful anticipation of a miracle finally realized. So, too, could I record the evidence of my progressing pregnancy—the early ultrasound images, the photos capturing my expanding girth—along with my reflections on the meaning of this so-common and yet so-personal experience.

The church played an integral part in my life throughout those months. Early on, I applied for an interim position editing my church's regional newspaper. To my surprise, despite having confided that I could work only until the baby arrived, I got the job. I also continued to freelance for my denomination's national newspaper and worked on the church's daily newspaper at its triennial national convention that summer. And so I have many memories of the support I received from co-workers—and of on-the-job challenges such as trying to balance a laptop on a disappearing lap—to accompany my visual "scraps," such as photos of the convention and the birth announcement that appeared in the newspaper I had edited.

When my son arrived on Labor Day, two-and-a-half weeks early, the doctor told me, "You had a lot of saints praying for you up in heaven, my friend." I had come close to an emergency C-section, but all was well.

Some of our earliest visitors were church friends and clergy. Our parish family, which had followed my pregnancy enthusiastically, quickly embraced newborn Carl. We celebrated the Thanksgiving for the Birth of a Child before our church congregation when he was two weeks old and baptized him at two months on All Saints' Sunday. He sat on my lap when I joined my fellow choristers in singing Christmas carols at our church's soup kitchen and posed as baby Jesus for the annual pageant.

Naturally, since Carl is a first child, we and others photographed him prodigiously. And so I had many images to illustrate the stories I wanted to tell in my scrapbook about the epiphany of parenthood.

Spiritual scrapbooks needn't just be baby books, of course. Many people keep faith albums—what some call "faithbooks"—that provide a sort of pho-

The thing about scrapbooking is, it's a priceless heirloom you're passing on to future generations that only you can do.

LISA BEARNSON

tographic record of their faith journeys. You can organize faith albums according to the church calendar, from Advent through the season of Pentecost. Or you might use a faith album to record spiritual growth through a formal program such as Alpha, a ten-week course offered by various denominations that explores Christian faith, or the Roman Catholic Rite of Christian Initiation for Adults. The advantage of the faith album over a regular family album is that it lets the scrapper concentrate on the spiritual significance of life's events. Some scrappers create a religious album around a specific theme or event—such as a retreat album—while others may find an album focused on a hobby such as gardening functions as a spiritual journal.

Scrapbooks also provide an opportunity for ministry and a way to highlight personal or church ministries. My friend Anne Lemay, a children's librarian and a deacon in her church, held a scrapbook party to benefit an overseas ministry. She also creates scrapbook pages to educate parishioners about her church's ministry with seafarers. Other scrappers create albums highlighting church youth events, recording congregational histories and educating their children about their faith.

When our minister left to accept another call overseas, our congregation gathered to create a scrapbook filled with memories of his ministry among us. We included pages from individual members and families, bits of church history, ministry overviews and photo spreads of parish celebrations and events, from the Shrove Tuesday "Jambalaya and Jazz" we held every year on the day before Lent began to parish cleanup days to the annual Blessing of the Animals in October. He received the album on the day he was officially installed in his new post. While he and his wife appreciated the album, it also proved a blessing for our congregation. Assembling the album provided an opportunity to gather together, mourn our loss, share our memories, give thanks for our bless-

Let this be recorded for a generation to come, so that a people yet unborn may praise the Lord.

PSALM 102:18

ings, enjoy the creativity of what for many was a new craft and fashion something positive out of our collective experience. Some left inspired to create their own family "heritage albums."

Telling our stories in this way is important. My church's national convention in 2003 actually endorsed a resolution asking all church members to learn how to tell their faith stories. Now, I understand the value of telling faith stories as part of our fulfillment of the Great Commission to tell everyone the good news of Christ. But like many people, I find the "E word" scary. Evangelism is fine in theory, but tell acquaintances about my faith? Not easily. Creating a spiritual scrapbook, however, lets you tell your faith story without feeling as though you are forcing your beliefs upon someone else. You discuss it naturally while you and your friends work on your albums. The completed album serves as a record of your faith story for those who examine it. And, of course, it provides a tool for your own continued reflection on your spiritual path.

Scrapbooks can be simple or fancy, large or small. Each is as unique as its creator and the story it tells. This book aims to show you or your congregation how to tell your unique faith stories through the fun and fulfilling art of scrapbooking. The section **Charting Your Faith Journey** provides guidance for chronicling your own spiritual life and that of your family, including how to create a wedding, baby or memorial faith scrapbook. **Building Community** offers advice on starting a church "crop club," completing a scrapbook as a congregational project and preserving church history in an album.

While I hope you will find the whole book helpful, don't feel obligated to read it in order. Depending on your scrapbooking goals or experience, you initially may want to focus on particular chapters or sections. If you're completely new to scrapbooking, you may find the final **Building Blocks** section, which describes basic scrapbook materials and page-design guidelines, especially helpful.

I wanted my girls to know the stories.

Robin Montgomery

Whatever your approach, have fun. Scrapbooking is enjoyable in many ways: as a creative outlet, a communal activity, a relaxation tool, a history project. Creating a faith album lets you explore and document your spirituality in a special way. Yes, this is a serious subject, but it's also a joyful one. In our ever-busier world, spiritual scrapbooking offers an opportunity for quiet reflection and new insights into God's importance and influence in our lives. It lets us join with friends and share our faith stories in community. And it provides a lasting record of our spiritual journeys, a witness of faith for the generations to come.

CHAPTER 2
THE MODERN SCRAPPER

... see, everything has become new!

—2 Cor 5:17

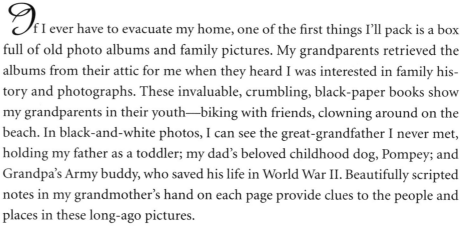

$\mathscr{I}$f I ever have to evacuate my home, one of the first things I'll pack is a box full of old photo albums and family pictures. My grandparents retrieved the albums from their attic for me when they heard I was interested in family history and photographs. These invaluable, crumbling, black-paper books show my grandparents in their youth—biking with friends, clowning around on the beach. In black-and-white photos, I can see the great-grandfather I never met, holding my father as a toddler; my dad's beloved childhood dog, Pompey; and Grandpa's Army buddy, who saved his life in World War II. Beautifully scripted notes in my grandmother's hand on each page provide clues to the people and places in these long-ago pictures.

Those albums begat others for my growing family "archives." My grandaunt supplied a box of pictures, carefully labeled. My mother-in-law contributed a wedding photo of my husband's grandmother, baby pictures of herself and my father-in-law, and other family mementoes. The most unusual item was a scrapbook assembled by my husband's paternal grandfather, Walter Hausman. The book itself is a legal-size bound ledger, such as an accountant might use, with a U.S. seal stamped into the cover. Inside, Walter pasted newspaper clippings, cartoons and the odd photo, with occasional handwritten notes on dates and events. The first page, for example, lists his Navy enlistment and discharge dates along with naval photos from a newspaper or magazine. Many pages include items without context—sayings such as "Loving a woman for her beauty is like eating a bird for its singing" and poems like *The Gamblers Will Get You*. Lost to history is the significance of photos of Argentine dancer Blanca Alvarez or the British lacrosse players defeating Harvard. Were they people he knew and events he attended, or merely items of interest he saw in the newspaper and decided to save?

The book provides a fascinating peek into the life of a man I never met. Yet it also highlights the shortcomings of albums before archival and decorative materials became readily available and before album "journaling" became the norm. The pages and their contents, dating from the 1920s, are mostly yellowed, and the items appear somewhat randomly on the pages, arranged where they'd fit. The album wasn't even, initially, a scrapbook: Bits of penciled columns of figures, letters and parts of names protrude from beneath some of the clippings, revealing that, in apparent thriftiness, Walter recycled the ledger for his album.

As Walter's album demonstrates, scrapbooking isn't new. A scrapbook timeline created by archivist Susan Tucker at Tulane University dates the craft's roots to ancient Greek and Roman tablets and to "emblem books" fashioned by medieval scribes (see "A Scrapbook Timeline" on page 119). Over the centuries, scrapbooking developed from Giorgio Vasari's art albums in the 1500s to "extra-illustrated books," which combined printed books with blank pages

The history of art is the history of revivals.

SAMUEL BUTLER
(1835–1902)[1]

for scrapping in the 1700s, to the "friendship albums" of the early nineteenth century. The term scrapbook was commonly used by 1825, and in 1872 Mark Twain began marketing his own patented "self-pasting" scrapbook.

Today's scrapbooks, however, *are* new. They may include newspaper clippings and other memorabilia, but photos typically take center stage. Decorative papers and stickers liven up the albums and can foster a thematic or cohesive look. The overall effect is of an enhanced photo album.

The theme underlying most contemporary scrapbooks is the desire to record family history. Enthusiasts stress the importance of listing the names of everyone in the album and journaling details of the events depicted, so future generations will understand their significance. Keeping those generations in mind, today's scrappers are more likely to use archival-quality materials, such as acid-free papers and adhesives that won't damage photos and lignin-free pages that won't turn yellow. (Pages containing lignin, a chemical component of wood, may become discolored or brittle over time.)

While today's scrapbooks encompass everything from family, baby and wedding albums to pet albums, vacation albums and school albums, the roots of this new take on an old craft reside within the religious community and particularly with two devout churchwomen: Marielen Christensen, a member of the Church of Jesus Christ of Latter-day Saints, or Mormons, and Rhonda Anderson, who worships at a Foursquare church, a Pentecostal denomination. Experts credit Marielen with launching the modern scrapbook movement, while Rhonda's independent efforts a decade later created an influential network of home consultants and a line of products that serve millions of album makers in at least a dozen countries.

Born in 1943, Marielen had assembled scrapbooks since childhood. The Mormons encourage members to trace and record family histories, and she created scrapbooks of all shapes and sizes chronicling her family's life. But she began changing scrapbook history in the 1970s, when the bishop of her local worship community in Utah asked her to help motivate other church members to work on their family "book of remembrances." To prepare to help others, Marielen reviewed her own albums and discovered problems: the awkwardness of having different-sized books in one collection, the way rubber cement eventually worked its way through the paper, the damaging effects of cellophane tape. She began looking for a durable, standard-size album that fit neatly on a shelf.

Marielen decided on three-ring binders to hold scrapbook pages slipped into protective plastic sleeves. She located clear corner mounts for photos and an acid-free glue. She contacted paper companies looking for acid-free paper, then available only in white and generally used for legal documents. She located less-acidic colored papers that she used to brighten her pages and developed a file-folder system for organizing photos and memorabilia. Using these tools, Marielen created albums for each of her five children, highlighting sad as well as joyous events. She included some of the last photos of her mother and even pictures of her mother's funeral. "We believe that we'll always be together again as families after this life," she explains. "It was an opportunity to explain death to the children."

Members of her church ward, or congregation, enthusiastically embraced Marielen's techniques and product ideas. Soon, she began speaking about scrapbooking to other church and social groups. In 1980, she displayed fifty of her albums in a booth at a World Conference on Records in Salt Lake City. The exhibit generated a whirlwind of interest—by the third day, she had answered so many questions she was losing her voice. She went home with the names of twenty-five hundred people interested in more information on basic scrap-

"Faithbooks" glorify God and increase our faith. That is the bottom-line goal of these albums.

RHONDA ANDERSON

booking steps. Soon afterward, she amassed even more names while staffing a booth at Brigham Young University's Campus Education Week in Provo.

In response, Marielen and her husband wrote and self-published an eighty-page booklet with page samples and tips on making memory books, writing personal histories, recording oral histories and organizing keepsake items. The five thousand copies they printed sold out in a year. The couple began marketing specially made scrapbook binders, glue, corner mounts and papers, which they sold at cost. (Initially, her husband resisted selling items at all because the scrapbooking promotion was a "church assignment.") The Christensens expanded from selling items in the back of their family clothing and school-supply business to running Keeping Memories Alive, a full-fledged scrapbook-supply store plus thriving mail-order business, in Spanish Fork, Utah. They launched a wholesale division to supply scrapbook stores opening around the country in 1993 and added a website in 1996.

Rhonda Anderson followed a similar path in founding Creative Memories, perhaps the best-known name in scrapbooking today. She grew up watching her mother create scrapbook albums for each of her children and took over the family album tradition herself at age fifteen. For Rhonda, who prefers the term "album-making" to "scrapbooking," her work is a way to pass on family beliefs, values and history. "It was never a craft to me," she says. "It was a valuable tradition."

Rhonda continued that tradition as she married, had children and adopted a child from India. Always, she used the same strap-hinged Webway albums her mother had bought. When Webway stopped selling them in stores, she became a mail-order customer.

In 1987, like Marielen, she was asked to share her album-making techniques at her church. Rhonda brought a small tip sheet and some of her family

My scrapbooks are my family's museums. This is where I hold our very most priceless pieces of memorabilia.

Lisa Bearnson

albums to the mothers' group at Faith Chapel, a Foursquare church in Billings, Montana. At the end, all forty mothers were clamoring for albums like hers. Five asked her to make the same album presentation in their homes.

So the former Tupperware lady began teaching home classes: showing her family albums, telling people how to get their photos out of shoeboxes and organized into scrapbooks, and collecting album orders. Overwhelmed by the response, she sought advice from a friend and lawyer at Christian Conciliation Service in Billings, which strives to resolve differences between family members and friends without going to court. She showed him her albums and described the classes she was teaching and the intense interest they were generating. He told her, "Rhonda, every day I have people in my office who have no hope. If only they had albums like these, where they could go back and see all of the positive things in their life. . . I know they wouldn't be in my office. Everyone needs to have albums just like this."

"Wow," Rhonda thought. "Save the world through photo albums."

Then came one of those apparently dream-dashing moments that in fact provided the key to pursuing her vision. Rhonda returned home to a postcard informing her that Webway was discontinuing the style of scrapbook albums she used. She panicked: "How can they discontinue an album that's going to save the world?"

She called the company, never thinking it was already after hours in St. Cloud, Minnesota. But Cheryl Lightle was working late and answered the phone. Rhonda learned the album she wanted wasn't the one targeted for discontinuation. More importantly, she connected with Cheryl, who invited her to visit St. Cloud and present her ideas. That summer, Rhonda signed a contract with Antioch Company, which had bought the Webway business, and Creative Memories was born. Cheryl became co-founder and president of the

I think sometimes the Lord has certain things that you are meant to do.

MARIELEN CHRISTENSEN

company. By mid-2005, more than ninety thousand consultants were selling Creative Memories scrapbook products and conducting home classes on photo preservation and album techniques.

For Rhonda, who's often called "Keeper of the Mission" at Creative Memories, the faith component of the albums remains primary. She describes that first phone contact with Cheryl as a "God moment." And that's precisely the sort of story she believes belongs in people's albums. Faith albums don't just record birthday parties, holiday celebrations and the first day of school; they describe God's influence in those events.

"'Faithbooks' glorify God and increase our faith. That is the bottom-line goal of these albums," she says. "It's looking for his hand in everything that we do and then pointing that out through our pictures and stories."

It's a message album makers around the world have taken to heart.

CHAPTER 3
A CHANCE FOR REFLECTION AND WITNESS

I will call to mind the deeds of the Lord;
I will remember your wonders of old.
I will meditate on all your work,
and muse on your mighty deeds.

—Ps 77: 11–12

I want to give them a voice.

DAWN DOWDY

About a decade ago, I attended a women's retreat at an Episcopal convent in Mendham, New Jersey. Our retreat leader asked us to draw a graph representing the ups and downs of our life, then to superimpose a second graph showing the highs and lows of our spiritual journey. It fascinated me to see how the two lines coincided, how strong ups and downs sometimes followed one another closely and how sometimes the lowest points in my life simultaneously represented high points in my spiritual development.

A few years later, I created a similar life graph while training to be a facilitator for the Disciples of Christ in Community program and, again, during my role as facilitator for a DOCC group at my church. Started at an Episcopal church, DOCC is a program now used by many denominations in which participants meet weekly to listen to a lecture on basic tenets of Christianity, then break up into small, confidential, facilitator-led groups to talk about their faith and the ways it applies to their lives and to the church. Sharing your "life graph" can feel daunting, even when you're just telling your story to a few supportive people. But it also gives you a good perspective on the path your life has taken and how that relates to the faith journeys of others.

Faith scrapbooks provide a similar opportunity for personal reflection. As Tennessee scrapbook consultant Sandy Schwalb describes it, "When you're working on your 'faithbooking' album, that's when you're really looking inside yourself."

New Jersey scrapper Anne Lemay's garden scrapbook functions as a faith album for her, and she has used it to help lead a church program examining personal Lenten journeys and where we find God in our lives. With her scrapbook as illustration, Anne talked about finding God in gardening, how she prays for people or works out problems in her life while doing routine tasks like digging and weeding. Scrapbooking is a similarly helpful act of "liturgy," she says. Engaging in such focused activities somehow frees the mind to contemplate other things.

Faith albums also let Christians share their stories, now and with future generations. Indeed, a faith scrapbook can be a powerful vehicle of witness for someone who ordinarily shies away from overt evangelism, not wanting to be seen as thrusting her faith upon others. California scrapbook consultant Dawn Dowdy, who leads classes on creating faith albums, describes her ministry as helping women find a voice to talk about their faith.

For some scrappers, a faith album is more like a family album with a deliberate spiritual dimension. People like Dawn, Rhonda Anderson and Sandra Joseph, who started Reminders of Faith to help people create scrapbooks recording God's faithfulness in their lives, encourage people to do more than record spiritually significant moments in their families' lives. They urge them to record God's influence in the everyday events of family life—birthday parties, the first day of school, a hike in the park. "If you look at your albums, and you only see what you did and not what you stood for, what are you leaving behind?" Dawn asks.

Over and over, faith scrappers stress the importance of telling the stories behind the photos—even limiting the page decorations in favor of the all-important journaling. Too often, observes Rhonda, believers never write about critical moments in their lives, such as when they came to know Jesus as their Savior; how the Lord brought them together with their spouse; how they experienced an amazing rescue or weathered a major adversity. "It really is amazing," Rhonda says, "just to see how people often don't record the very things that do give us hope for the future."

Of course, every faith album, like every person's faith, is unique. And there are many different ways to organize a faith scrapbook.

I tend to organize all my albums chronologically. When I started my first scrapbook in February 2002, I began with photos of my son's second Christmas, just past, and worked forward. Because I naturally organize my albums this way, and because I come from a religious tradition that follows the seasons, feast days and commemorations of the church year, I find the church calendar an ideal organizing tool for a faith album. From the Advent wreath to the Epiphany star, the ashes heralding the start of Lent to the lilies of Easter, the church calendar offers ample inspiration for photos and spiritual reflections. And while the typical family album might include only the highlights of Christmas and Easter, a scrapbook based on the church calendar invites ruminations on religious events throughout the year, from the angel Gabriel's announcement that Jesus will be born to the coming of the Holy Spirit at Pentecost, from St. Peter's confession that Jesus is the Christ to the commemorations of various saints and church leaders.

Just because the church year starts with Advent, of course, doesn't mean you must start a faith scrapbook with that season. It's okay to begin elsewhere in the church year—just continue forward from there. In fact, I've heard scrapbook consultants advise novices to begin their first album with current photos. This lets you record details while they're fresh in your mind and helps you feel good that you're keeping up-to-date. You always can go back later to create an album with older or even historic photos.

Other scrappers and consultants suggest other ways to organize a personal faith album. Here are a few ideas.

Use the Scriptures, hymns or other devotional writings for inspiration. Some scrappers organize albums alphabetically, with an appropriate Bible verse and coordinating photograph for each page. The letter M, for example, might feature musical notations and the verse "Make a joyful noise unto the Lord," accompanied by a photo of a choir singing, children happily beating time with wooden spoons on pots and pans, a kitten mewing or friends laughing and splashing at the beach.

Consider choosing a poem, psalm, hymn or prayer, highlighting one line or verse per page. The well-known prayer attributed to Saint Francis, for example, offers the chance to reflect on your calling as peacemaker in the world ("Lord, make me an instrument of thy peace . . ."). The hymn *Earth and All*

I think the books are actually so perfect for strengthening faith because you can see right there in your pictures what blessings you have.

PATRICE KEALY

Stars offers wonderful visual images that lend themselves to photos and commentary on the wonders of God's world and how all glorify their Creator (". . . flowers and trees. . . loud blowing snowstorms. . . athlete and band. . . sing to the Lord a new song!").

Explore the meaning of a particular passage or lesson of Scripture, such as the Beatitudes, the fruits of the Spirit, the Ten Commandments or Paul's poetic depiction of love in First Corinthians ("Love is patient; love is kind . . ."). Or simply use Scripture verses meaningful to you that illustrate God at work in your life.

For New Jersey scrapbook consultant Patrice Kealy, using the Scriptures to create a spiritual scrapbook helped show her husband how her faith relates to their family life. Inspired by Rhonda Anderson, she gathered photos, matched them with appropriate Bible verses and gave the album to her spouse. "Keep traveling steadily along his pathway, and in due season he will honor you with every blessing" accompanies a picture of one of their children riding his bicycle. "I can do all things in him who strengthens me," reads the caption for a photo of a youngster paddling a canoe.

The visual aid of the photographs helped Patrice make the connection between the Scriptures and real life. And having the book in hand helped her answer her husband's question after his father died, a few years after her mother died of cancer: How are you able to get through this with your faith?

Through the scrapbook, she showed him how the words of the Bible applied to circumstances in their lives—and therefore how they could depend on God to help them through tough times, as the Scriptures promised. "It was easier to show him in pictures: 'Well, this is what's being said here, and this is what happened to us at this time, and look at this. It's real, it's true. So depend on that. You can count on God here.'"

When you're working on your "faithbooking" album, that's when you're really looking inside yourself.

SANDY SCHWALB

Create an ongoing prayer book. Christians are called to lives of prayer, at all times and in all places. A prayer scrapbook, Dawn explains, lets you record your prayers and the ways they are answered on facing pages. Instead of being completed all at once, such an album invites you to return again and again to detail how God guided you, blessed you or solved a problem that you raised in prayer, and then to write additional prayers.

After hearing Christina Lando speak about her plans to serve as a missionary to Bulgaria, for example, Dawn titled a page in her album "God equips those he calls." She asked God to bless Christina and the fund-raising event she was embarking on in preparation for her missionary work, and she thanked God for Christina and her faith. On the facing page, which features a photo of the missionary, Dawn later recorded her thanks that Christina had met her financial goal and asked God to be with her as she traveled to Bulgaria for training. On another page, Dawn placed a photo of her three young children and asked God to look after them, to bring them closer to God each day and to ensure that their future spouses also would come to the Lord. The blank facing page waits for the day she can mount photos of her new children-in-law and describe God's answer to her prayer.

Such an approach also is a good way to place our aspirations before God— our life goals (finding a new home or job; coping with a parent's illness; improving grades at school; learning to play an instrument; establishing an exercise program) and our spiritual goals (serving the poor at the soup kitchen; completing a Bible study; cultivating virtues such as patience or kindness; enriching our prayer life; starting a new ministry; singing God's praises in the choir). At Patrice's church, she is preparing a scrapbook in which parishioners can enter prayer requests along with photographs to help make the names meaningful to those who may not know the people whose names are lifted in prayer during worship services.

Create a "turning points" album. Lisa Bearnson, author and founding editor of *Creating Keepsakes Magazine*, keeps an old doll's head on the shelf of her office as a reminder of a lesson she learned in fourth grade. Christmas was approaching, and she anxiously lobbied her mother for the perfect gift in the toy catalogue: a doll's head with hair that she could style and curl. Repeatedly, she showed her mother the doll heads in the book, pointing out the beautiful one she wanted and the ugly one she didn't.

Christmas morning, she recalls, "to my utter shock and dismay, I got the ugly one. I ran to my bedroom and cried and cried and cried." Hours later, the family went out to dinner, and she saw her mother's eyes were as red and swollen as her own. In that moment, she realized how much mothers must do to prepare for Christmas and how unappreciative she had been of her mother's efforts. "Right then and there, I vowed that I would be appreciative [of] everything that I got in life. I'm forty-one. I keep that doll head on my shelf to this day as a reminder."

Sixth grade brought another revelation. She had discovered it was easier to tap the boy sitting in front of her at school to copy his answers than to study. "I had him trained; he must have had a crush on me."

But one night, lying in bed, she thought of her Savior and his perfect life, and that she wouldn't be worthy to be with her Heavenly Father if she died. She got on her knees and prayed. Then she woke her sister, told her story and prayed with her. Her sister helped her type a note to her teacher, confessing and vowing never to cheat again—a promise she's kept.

Lisa created a scrapbook of these and other turning points in her life, including pictures of objects such as the doll's head that represent those epiphanies.

Such an album could include profound revelations of joy as well. I once experienced a transcendent moment of God's presence during a Communion service while on retreat. In my lowest, most depressed and anxious moments,

If you look at your albums, and you only see what you did and not what you stood for, what are you leaving behind?

DAWN DOWDY

that experience remains a touchstone for me, my rock-bottom proof that God exists. This kind of story belongs in a "turning points" album, alongside photographs of the sanctuary in that monastery.

Quitting a job, launching a ministry, having a child, seeing someone overcome a handicap, getting married or divorced, joining a new church, surviving cancer—all are examples of critical turning points to consider including in a faith album. Such a scrapbook highlights the important moments and changes in your life and helps you chart your faith journey.

Similarly, Rhonda suggests listing the ten most influential people in your life and journaling about the ways they influenced you. Looking back at those who most affected you through the years shows how you grew and changed. It also highlights the importance of relationships in our lives, and how we're all interconnected as part of the body of Christ.

Create a gratitude album. Use a scrapbook to count your blessings. Consider using the alphabet, featuring one letter on each page to highlight what you're grateful for. The page for letter C might show photos of your children or your church. Letter S might give thanks for sunrises or stars or a favorite saint. Anne Fraley, a minister in Tennessee, comments that this is a fun way to use pictures that don't fit in other albums and to remember life's more ordinary blessings, such as blueberries.

Whatever method you use, what's important is that your faith album truly reflects you and your values, and that you choose a scrapbook format that's meaningful and comfortable for you.

For Anne Fraley, the faith life she personally experiences naturally intersects with the faith lives of others because of her job. So the pages chronicling her ministry include a list of the people she buried while serving as a priest at a St. Louis church and a photo of a columbarium sculpture (a vault with niches

It really is amazing just to see how people often don't record the very things that do give us hope for the future.

RHONDA ANDERSON

for holding cremated remains) there created by a member who died. "As a priest, what I will 'scrap' is going to be different," she says. "No one else is probably going to have a picture of a columbarium in their book."

When my grandmother Dorothy died, the minister remarked in her homily that her passing left a Dorothy-sized hole. Each of us is unique, with a unique path to follow and a unique witness to offer. No one else can fill our "hole." Creating a faith album gives you insight into your own irreplaceable story and helps you to tell it, as a reminder to yourself of the spiritual path you've followed and as a witness to those who come after you.

For Reflection and Journaling

- How did your faith journey begin? Did you grow up in the church, or did you come to know Christ later in life?

- Who nurtured your faith? Which family members, friends, ministers or mentors influenced your spiritual growth?

- What are the important spiritual turning points in your life?

- What have you learned about God and God's work in your life?

Dear Lord,
   For eyes to see the world's wonders,
   I thank you.
   For guidance upon our path of life, and the wisdom to follow it,
   I thank you.
   For the many helpmates you provide to accompany us on our journeys,
   I thank you.

For hands to create a lasting memorial to your glory,
I thank you.
For fun and friendship in working together,
    and quiet contemplation while working alone,
I thank you.
Please bless me now as I trace my faith through the pages of this scrapbook,
and inspire my creativity in using this craft to tell your story.
    Amen.

CHAPTER 4
RECORDING THE JOURNEY

. . . give me understanding, that I may
learn your commandments.

—Ps 119:73

*M*y faith always been an important part of my life—but I've been more
spiritually attuned at some times than at others. Sometimes, it seemed I just
went through the motions of going to church every Sunday. Sometimes, doubts
and fears filled my mind. At other times, I saw God at work in my life every-
where and felt wonderfully close to him. Sometimes I've prayed, well, reli-
giously; at other times, sporadically. I like to think I'm becoming more faithful
as time passes, but I suspect there's an ebb and flow to everyone's spiritual life.

Certain things, however, seem to increase my spiritual focus. Times of
great joy or sadness can spark significant spiritual growth. Similarly, times of
deliberate study can bring new spiritual discipline and insight.

Scrapbooking as part of a Christian formation program can be a powerful
tool in chronicling your spiritual path and recording your thoughts as you go

through the process. You can create a faith album as you undertake such a program at any point along your faith journey, from an inquirers' or Confirmation class as you contemplate joining a church to a Bible study or ministry-preparation course offered by your congregation to a formal discernment process and seminary studies.

Many congregations offer formation programs for adults who want to join their church or to deepen their spiritual lives, from the Rite of Christian Initiation for Adults (RCIA) in the Roman Catholic Church to the Disciples of Christ in Community (DOCC) and Alpha courses used by various denominations.

In RCIA, adults meet regularly and learn about the Catholic faith. Pat Hope, who leads RCIA at a church in New Jersey, prefers the term *process* rather than *program* because the goal is to help students begin a relationship with God, "and that never ends." Such a process naturally lends itself to journaling, an important element in faith scrapbooking. In a faith album, RCIA participants could recount their faith journey leading to the Roman Catholic Church and record lessons learned about the church and its teachings—including reflections and questions about those lessons. They could transcribe significant Scripture passages or other quotations from the study materials. And those who decide to join the church could describe their feelings about receiving the sacraments.

Such an album probably would be more word-centered than photo-centered, especially since the church may prohibit photographing worship services or certain parts of the sanctuary. That's fine, especially for a faith album, whose focus is providing a record of your walk with God, not displaying pretty pages. Meaningful pictures for this type of album might include exterior shots of the church; pictures of significant people encountered on the path to the church, such as a spouse or member of the clergy; and photos of religious

I sought the Lord, and he answered me, and delivered me from all my fears.

Psalm 34:4

items or symbols such as a Bible, cross, gravestone, baptismal font, bread and wine, Advent wreath, Easter lily or lamb. Similarly, students in an adult inquirers' class or Confirmation class could use a scrapbook to journal and record their reflections as they prepare to make a greater commitment to their church.

Some church programs, such as DOCC and Alpha (a ten-week course featuring supper followed by talks and discussion of key issues relating to Christian faith), help believers and seekers examine questions of faith and its relevance to everyday life. Some, such as Lenten programs and Bible and book studies, delve short-term into the meaning of particular texts or issues. Others, such as Education for Ministry (EFM), provide an intense, long-term study of the Bible and personal faith that often leads students into new areas of ministry. (Similar to DOCC, EFM began in an Episcopal seminary but now is used by multiple denominations.) Still other courses prepare students for a particular type of ministry, such as chaplaincy work or lay pastoral care. Ongoing small groups provide spiritual nourishment in many congregations.

All of these formation programs lend themselves to scrapbooking your reflections and experiences throughout the process. Several years ago, I participated in a Spiritual Formation Group using James Bryan Smith's *A Spiritual Formation Workbook*. Our small group met weekly to learn about various spiritual disciplines, then committed to a task exercising one of those disciplines during the week. At the next meeting, we reported on how we'd fared.

Scrappers participating in this program could record reflections on the process, their prayers and their weekly commitments and how they did or didn't achieve them. They could include photographs of people they pray for or activities they tackle as spiritual exercises. Later, they could look back at the album to review their progress and their spiritual strengths and weaknesses, and to remind themselves of what they learned during the program.

Take my life and let it be consecrated, Lord, to thee; take my moments and my days, let them flow in ceaseless praise.

THE HYMNAL 1982

Participants in a spiritual-renewal program such as Cursillo (Spanish for "little course") similarly could record how it deepened their faith. Roman Catholic laymen started Cursillo in Spain in 1944, and various Christian denominations subsequently adopted and adapted the program, sometimes under other names, such as the Methodist Walk to Emmaus. Designed to bring people closer to Christ and help them understand their individual callings as Christian leaders, Cursillo begins with a three-day weekend that may include personal testimonies, discussions, social activities, music, meditation and worship. The weekend can lead to "that kind of faith conversion experience where you realize, 'Wow, this is the awesome God,'" Cursillo graduate Anna Notation-Rhoades told me. Afterward, people want to share their Cursillo experience, and they continue to meet with other graduates—called Cursillistas—to bolster their commitments to God and the church.

Creating a Cursillo scrapbook could capture the excitement of that "conversion." Cursillistas could record how they were approached and sponsored for a weekend and their experiences during that time. Cursillo reunions and follow-up activities would provide them with continuing scrapbook opportunities for reflecting on that "awesome God" and what they are doing in God's service.

You also can create a scrapbook highlighting one exercise in a spiritual formation program. EFM, for example, is a four-year course that includes writing an annual spiritual autobiography. This assignment is an ideal opportunity for creating a small scrapbook. Chances are, finding appropriate pictures and relating them to your faith story will spark memories you wouldn't have had if you'd simply composed your autobiography at the computer or with pen and ink.

Those pursuing further religious studies at a seminary can use a scrapbook to record their spiritual growth through those years. An album offers a

It's a wonderful place to go to remember the people who have been a part of your personal journey.

Judy Carter

place to assimilate what you're learning and feeling, what it's like to live in a seminary community and your dreams and fears for the future. For those who enjoy losing themselves in creative endeavors, scrapbooking can be a welcome respite from the rigors of study and service.

Sometimes, a seminarian's spouse creates a scrapbook about those years. He or she might record the spouse's experiences, as scrapbook consultant Judy Carter did. She assembled two volumes mapping her husband's faith journey—from his first call to ordained ministry to his response to that call in his fifties to his seminary days in Texas and first year in ordained ministry in Georgia.

But a seminarian's spouse also might record his or her own experiences, or the family's spiritual growth, during that time. Anna, a scrapbook consultant, relocated with her husband and their three children to Tennessee so her husband could attend a seminary there. Seminarians called to ordained ministry, she comments, have concrete milestones marking their formation journey: their call, the creation of their discernment committee, various approvals in their steps toward ordination, the move to seminary. Spouses also go through a formation process during this time, but its milestones are less obvious, she says. "The spouse winds up being the one who has to be willing to make all the adjustments without . . . all the excitement."

Scrapbooking has proved valuable in helping Anna chart her own milestones in the seminary process, and it provides a touchstone when times get tough. She likes looking back in her album at a poem from a worship service about the journey of being a seminary spouse, thinking, "Now I'm in the middle of the poem," and having an inkling of what will happen next. Looking through the scrapbook, she finds it very moving to recall how volunteer seminarians unpacked their truck when they arrived. The first person they met in the "moving crew" was a seminarian from Alaska whose wife was a good friend

Your word is a lamp to my feet and a light to my path.

PSALM 119:105

*Give ear, O my people,
to my teaching;
incline your ear to the
words of my mouth.*

PSALM 78:1

of Anna's Cursillo sponsor. "That's all part of how we sustain ourselves when we can't see God working so clearly," she says.

She's also recorded her children's experiences and reflections. In a Kids of Seminarians group, for example, one of her children wrote down the things he liked best and least about his dad attending seminary. That's in her scrapbook, along with the story of the frog her five-year-old discovered in their toilet the morning after they arrived. The ritual of photographing and freeing the frog helped bind them together as a family in their new home. Through the scrapbook, the children can rekindle memories of the frog rescue and of their godmother helping them move. "It's neat for the kids to have a picture of Auntie Barb actually falling asleep on the top of a box."

While very intense at the time, experiences such as attending seminary or participating in another spiritual formation program often pass quickly. In time, we lose the intensity of those thoughts and experiences. A scrapbook helps preserve those memories. It also shows us the steps of our spiritual development: the things we discovered, the challenges we overcame, the highs and lows of our lives and how they relate to the peaks and valleys of our faith journey. We can see how much we've grown spiritually, how we've acquired new leadership skills and taken on new responsibilities in God's service and where God may be calling us to future ministry.

For Reflection and Journaling

- Why did you enroll in a spiritual formation program? What do you hope to learn or experience?

- What are you discovering about God?

- What lessons surprise you? Challenge you?

- How are you putting your new knowledge into practice? How are you making your faith relevant in your life?

Ever-wise God, source of all knowledge,

    You give us teachers throughout out lives to help us learn your ways. Bless the leaders of this program as they share their knowledge with us. Bless me as I read and learn and discuss and listen. Give me a discerning mind and heart as I seek to understand more about you and your church. And help me to put my new knowledge to good use, as I seek to follow you and minister to others.

    Amen.

CHAPTER 5
WEDDING BELLS

"For this reason a man shall leave his father and mother and
be joined to his wife, and the two shall become one flesh"

—Matthew 19:5; NRSV, Anglicized Edition

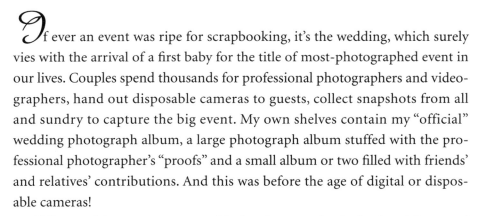

*I*f ever an event was ripe for scrapbooking, it's the wedding, which surely vies with the arrival of a first baby for the title of most-photographed event in our lives. Couples spend thousands for professional photographers and videographers, hand out disposable cameras to guests, collect snapshots from all and sundry to capture the big event. My own shelves contain my "official" wedding photograph album, a large photograph album stuffed with the professional photographer's "proofs" and a small album or two filled with friends' and relatives' contributions. And this was before the age of digital or disposable cameras!

When making arrangements with the photographer beforehand, I stressed two things: getting pictures of all the family and friends attending, and photographing certain especially meaningful elements at the church—the altar flowers my mother arranged; our college buddy seated at the organ; me and my husband standing beside the 250-plus-year-old steeple, removed for safety and awaiting repairs. In other words, I wanted to preserve the sacred place and the parts we played in it as well as the sacred ceremony. And I wanted to memorialize those vital relationships—from childhood friends to far-flung family members to college cronies—accompanying us to that day.

Nearly twenty years later, I realize what those photographs lack is context. I know why the steeple's sitting there and who arranged the flowers. I can muse about the poignancy of the wedding photos of my husband and me with our four grandmas and one grandpa. The first children in our families to wed, my husband and I were the last to have all of those grandparents at our ceremony. But those memories remain stored in my head, invisible to others picking up the photo albums. That's why I plan to move those "proofs" into a scrapbook. I want to caption those photos, tell some of those stories and provide a record for those who follow.

For many of today's brides, a wedding scrapbook is a first step, not a twenty-year-old afterthought. I've given two scrapbook kits as wedding gifts. This provides a chance to capture the feelings and meaning as well as the details of the moment. It's a perfect opportunity to reflect on the spiritual as well as celebrative side: the vows and Scripture passages you chose, the place you wed, the loved ones who witnessed your commitment, what "holy matrimony" means for you and your spouse.

Katherine McGlynn of Utah created an album of her wedding, where the role of the church in which she married seemed preordained. When she started dating her future husband, they attended different churches. But before their engagement, they began attending church together. After their betrothal, they discovered one set of her grandparents and one set of his had married there. So where else would they wed?

Not surprisingly, the church takes center stage in Katherine's wedding scrapbook. Other pages trace the couple's journey, from engagement to hon-

*Love is patient;
love is kind;
love is not envious
or boastful or
arrogant or rude.*

1 Corinthians 13:4

eymoon, but the events at the church form the focal point: the rehearsal, the rehearsal dinner, the wedding itself. Guests scattered throughout the church photographed the event from various angles. One album page details how the couple found the church together, why they liked it, why they stayed. "We're very connected to the church," says Katherine.

Of course, weddings in nonchurch venues can be equally meaningful. As a wedding gift, Anne Fraley "scrapped" album pages from a marriage ceremony she attended on a beach. The couple wrote their own vows, and the scrapbook pages include the vows as well as a photo of the bride copying them from her journal to carry to the ceremony.

Healing through Scrapbooking

Assembling a wedding album provides a valuable time for reflection—even if the marriage failed.

Scrapbook consultant Carole Ann King of New Jersey was preparing for her son's wedding in London and feeling anxious about spending three days with her ex-husband and his wife during the festivities. She found herself thinking about her own wedding to her son's father.

"I had never put the wedding album together because the marriage was so chaotic," she says. But she still had the pictures.

She decided to create a small gift album for her son. "I wanted Morgan to see that there was a time when his father and I were very happy and that he came from a situation of love and happiness." She also wanted to give her son's German bride a sense of his family heritage.

Carole Ann chose only happy photos from the wedding and early days of her marriage—the bride walking down the aisle with her dad, the happy couple at the reception, a tiny Morgan and his father, the now-deceased grandparents on both sides who would have been so proud of their grandson. She secured them in the album and added simple decorations. Then she captioned each picture, writing as though addressing her son. Near the first picture in the church she wrote: "See how happy your mom and your grandfather were walking me down the aisle." For a reception photo of her and her ex-husband standing, arms around each other's waists, she joked: "Hang on! It's going to be a bumpy ride." For another photo of her ex-husband, the victim of serious illness since then, she wrote: "See how handsome your father was, and how healthy."

While she worked on the album, late into the night, a transformation occurred. "I felt happy and calm in my thoughts instead of all that bitterness."

After a divorce, you tend to focus on the negative, she says. But creating the scrapbook focused her on the positive memories. Thirty-four years later, she reflected on that marriage from a new perspective and found healing. "I let the Holy Spirit take me wherever she wanted. It was a spiritual journey."

Carole Ann no longer felt nervous about meeting her ex. In London, she presented the album before the rehearsal dinner. It helped everyone relax and provided a healing moment as well between Morgan—age five when his parents separated—and his father.

Scrapbooks provide a valuable space for spiritual reflection on this life-changing event, even when assembled years later. Here are some ways to approach a wedding album.

Get organized. Sort photos by topic—rehearsal dinner, pre-ceremony preparations, the service, the reception, the sendoff. Think about the events that were most meaningful or most unique for your occasion. Did you wear your grandmother's antique necklace? Did you meet your spouse at church? Did you sign a family Bible? Did you write the vows?

My beloved speaks and says to me: "Arise, my love, my fair one, and come away."

SONG OF SOLOMON 2:10

Consider adding engagement and honeymoon photos, as Katherine did, or even pictures showing you setting up housekeeping together. This lets you reflect on your whole journey, how God brought you together and where you hope to go next.

Collect the data. Jot down special memories, anecdotes, mishaps, "God moments," people's names—all those details so easily lost. Consider adding others' stories or, if you're planning your album before the wedding, having guests sign album pages or journaling boxes (small pieces of lined or unlined paper that can be mounted in the scrapbook later). Gather the memorabilia you want to include—cards, invitations, programs, business cards, ribbons. Perhaps you'd like to incorporate photographs of your parents' and in-laws' weddings or baby pictures of you and your spouse.

Assemble your book. You might decorate the pages ahead of time or as you go along, but use common colors or titles or stickers to provide a cohesive look. Consider using parts of the wedding vows or Scripture verses on each page.

Journal. Depending on your style, you might prefer shorter captions or longer narratives. But don't just stick with names and dates, as important as those are. Reflect on the meaning of the wedding venue, be it a church with personal and family history as it was for Katherine or an outdoor setting that calls to mind God's grandeur. Talk about how God brought you and your spouse together, the significance of the vows you wrote or the Scripture passages and music you chose.

Think about telling stories the photos don't tell. When Anne assembled an album page featuring photos from the bridesmaids' luncheon preceding a wedding at which she officiated, the key wasn't the pictures but the story behind them. She wrote: "The setting and exquisite food were notable, of course, but what made the occasion most special was the tribute Carrie paid to her brides-

O God, you have so consecrated the covenant of marriage that in it is represented the spiritual unity between Christ and his Church.

Book of Occasional Services[2]

maids. Along with a gift of thanks to each for being part of her wedding, she had written a personal note describing why she valued the friendship she had with each of her 'maids, affirming and celebrating the person and the friendship. Naturally, tears flowed in abundance. Carrie's graciousness, thoughtfulness and love for those dear to her were readily apparent, and no surprise!"

Write from today's perspective. If you're newly married, think back on how you met and describe how you felt on your wedding day. But if you're assembling a book years later, don't try to re-enter the mind of the new bride. When you discuss the wedding guests, reflect on those relationships. Who were they, yes, but why were they important to you? What's happened to them since? What does it mean to you to see their pictures in your album?

Reflect on your marriage. How has your love held you together through the years? Or, if your marriage ended, what lessons did you learn? As Carole Ann discovered, this reflective process can be very healing. (See "Healing through Scrapbooking" on page 34).

Reassembling an old photo album into a scrapbook can have an added practical advantage. My own "proofs" sit in a magnetic album, which damages photos over time. So moving them to a scrapbook not only will give me a chance to record wedding memories and reflect on the spiritual journey of marriage, but it also will help ensure my wedding pictures can live happily ever after.

For Christians, weddings are more than a legality or a social occasion; they're a sacrament, an "outward and visible sign of an inward and spiritual reality." Creating a spiritual wedding album lets you reflect on the sacred nature of your union and on the community of faithful people who witnessed your vows and share your life. Its pages bear testament to your love and faith, long after the wedding flowers have faded.

The joys of marriage are the heaven on earth . . .

JOHN FORD
(1586–1639)[3]

For Reflection and Journaling

- How did you choose the location for your wedding? What special significance does it hold for you?

- What was your wedding ceremony like? Why did you choose particular Scripture passages, readings or hymns?

- What people were instrumental in bringing you and your spouse together? In helping you plan the wedding? Who participated in the ceremony? How are these people important in your life?

- What is the spiritual meaning of marriage for you? How do you and your spouse hope to live out your faith together?

God of love,

I thank you for the great gift of my spouse, _____. Thank you for guiding us along our separate paths in life, until we met and joined together in a new family. Please bless our marriage as you blessed that long-ago wedding in Cana.

Guide me now as I recall our meeting and joining, our plans and dreams, our friendship and love. Help me to tell the story of our union, and of the faith that is its foundation, in the pages of this scrapbook.

I ask this in the name of Jesus, our ever-loving companion.

Amen.

CHAPTER 6
MIRACULOUS BEGINNINGS

'For this child I prayed; and the Lord has
granted me the petition that I made to him.'

—1 Sam 1:27

*I*f ever we feel a sense of the miraculous, it's when a child is born. I remember feeling as though my face actually glowed for days after my son's arrival. I'd look in the mirror and see, not an exhausted, sore, puffy-faced woman, but a face blooming with joy and wonder and peace—the same look I'd spied with surprise when I'd glimpsed myself during a spiritual retreat.

When we gaze at our newborns, we see God and all the possibilities of God in the world. But early motherhood is, to paraphrase Dickens, the best of times and the worst of times, as raging hormones, sleepless nights and that "oh-Lord-now-what-do-I-do" feeling take their toll. The emotions are so intense they seem impossible to forget, yet the days are so hectic they soon blur into the new challenges that follow. I remember frantically recording the details of Carl's birth during my occasional fifteen minutes of freedom from baby care so I wouldn't forget. My husband and I also snapped enough pictures to fill several photo albums and make the face of the local photo-store proprietor light up every time we walked in the door.

Those photos and descriptions proved invaluable when I finally began assembling my baby scrapbook. Unlike the traditional baby books I had (mostly) maintained, this album followed my spiritual journey into parenthood. The lagtime between birth and album-making—in my case, several years—let me reflect back on what had happened and how it had changed me. The photos and journal entries provided insight into how I felt initially. The sacraments and seasons of church life—baptism, Christmas, Shrove Tuesday celebration, Holy Week and Easter—provided a framework for telling the story of my son's early days. When Carl looks through the album, he will see how eagerly his family awaited him, how his church family embraced him and how much our faith and church have been part of his life from the beginning.

Some parents create albums to provide a sense of family for adopted children. Some adoption agencies, in fact, require families to create such a scrapbook as part of the adoption process. Rhonda Anderson describes how, when she and her husband adopted the first of two children from India, she ran out to get the same sort of album for her new daughter as she had used for her biological children.

Adoption albums can establish family history and show how a child's arrival answers parents' prayers. Creating such a scrapbook also can help parents reflect on their unique path to parenthood.

On you I was cast
from my birth,
and since my mother
bore me you have
been my God.

PSALM 22:10

Building Families

While some families create albums for their adopted children, scrapbooks also can be invaluable in enabling an adoption to happen. Crisis Pregnancy Outreach near Tulsa, Oklahoma, for example, ministers to single pregnant girls and women and, if they wish, arranges open adoptions for their babies. Director Cheryl Bauman's credo is that the Christian nonprofit agency is finding families for babies, not babies for families, and scrapbooks play an integral part in making the matches. Prospective adoptive families create albums that describe themselves and their faith. Each mother-to-be tells Cheryl what she desires in the family adopting her baby—a home in-state or out-of-state, a household with pets, parents belonging to a particular denomination, the presence or lack of other siblings—and Cheryl shows her the albums meeting her criteria. The mother selects an adoptive family based on the life stories told in these albums.

While I found this ministry inspiring when I learned about it, I realized that my conversation with Cheryl had been a true "God incident" when my husband and I decided some months later that we wanted to adopt a newborn. We learned that many adoption agencies now require profiles from prospective parents to help birth mothers choose who will raise their babies, and the agency we chose welcomed my desire to create a family scrapbook as our profile. Today, I'm busily planning an album that will showcase our family and its values, including the importance of faith and our church community in our lives. God willing, we soon will become parents again, aided in our quest by the creation of this special form of spiritual scrapbook.

Like wedding albums, baby albums don't need to record only the happy or easy times. Dawn Dowdy used them to chronicle one of the toughest times in her life.

Derek Dowdy entered the world in 1998 at 2 pounds 4 ounces on the day his mother was supposed to start Lamaze class. He remained in the hospital for six weeks, with Dawn anxiously watching every twitch and wiggle. She saw other mothers holding last rites for their premature infants. "I really didn't know from one moment to the next if he was going to make it. I was scared to death I was going to lose him."

But Dawn didn't lose him; today, Derek is a healthy youngster. In those early, uncertain days, however, Dawn snapped photo after photo of her tiny baby. She later assembled them into two albums chronicling Derek's first weeks and her own spiritual journey through that frightening time. Providing visual continuity, Dawn mounted banners of periwinkle-blue and vellum paper, left to right, at the top of each page. Then she added religious inspirational stickers and her own prayers and Bible verses. She asked the Lord for strength and thanked him for keeping the family together.

Creating the albums took years. The process provided healing and closure, but the photos also brought back overwhelming emotions. Working on the albums, Dawn felt great thankfulness and a certainty that her suffering had a purpose. "The Lord wanted me to stay close to him because of what the future may hold. He wanted me to be stronger, and I feel grateful for that."

Since then, she has helped several other women who delivered premature babies. She believes that's why she went through what she did with Derek—to give strength and grace to these other women.

Creating a baby album may seem like an insurmountable task for any new mother, let alone one struggling through the red tape of adoption procedures or the frightening world of the neonatal intensive care unit. But there are ways to make the job easier and to lay the groundwork in case you, like me, wait a few years to start.

Think about buying supplies and even decorating the album ahead of time. You can place color-coordinated paper or ribbon borders across the top or bottom or down the sides. Matching titles also help provide a cohesive look. You can buy album pages with titles already on them or create your own titles, adding special entries such as "first trip to church" or "meeting the minister" to standards such as "first visitors" and "first birthday." Add a few decorative stickers, or keep them nearby to use after you complete each page. Be sure to leave plenty of room to insert photos and journal your stories after the baby arrives.

If even decorating an album while preparing for the baby seems daunting, ask a friend or relative to help—or hint that you'd like such a scrapbook. Some scrappers predecorate albums as baby gifts, helping the busy new mother get organized and saving her much of the detailed work. Others enlist a group to decorate pages, perhaps as a baby-shower or preshower activity.

Organize photos and memorabilia. Set up a simple system of envelopes or folders into which you can slip shower invitations, birth announcements, cards, photographs and other items as soon as you get them. Label the files and keep them in order, whether chronologically or by topic, so you quickly can pull one out and mount the items in your album.

If you don't keep a journal, jot down notes of stories or facts you want to include and add them to the appropriate file. If you want to record information on the back of photographs, be sure to use a photo-safe marker or pencil. (The ink in an ordinary pen can leak through over time.) Be sure to press lightly, so the indentation won't show through on the front.

Once the baby arrives, divide album-making into steps. Spend ten minutes cropping photos while supervising baby's daily "tummy time" lying on his

[H]e blesses your children within you.

PSALM 147:13

or her stomach. (As an infant, Carl protested mightily over this muscle-building exercise that's so important now that we put babies to sleep on their backs to prevent Sudden Infant Death Syndrome. A little cropping would have been a welcome distraction!) Add adhesive strips to cropped pictures while watching television. When you have a bit more time, spread out the photos and decide which go together on each page. Then keep those sets of photos together. Assembling a page doesn't take long when the photos are cropped, you know which ones belong together and all you need to do is remove the adhesive's backing and attach the photos to the page. Reserve journaling for quiet moments such as baby's naptime, when you can reflect on the pictures and the story you want to tell.

Consider organizing the album by religious milestones: dedication ceremonies, baptisms, special worship services and church celebrations. Later, you could expand the album beyond a baby book to include other highlights of your child's spiritual journey, such as First Communion, Confirmation, mission trips and ministry experiences.

Include a family tree or a brief family history. This may be especially meaningful for a child entering a family by adoption, but all children like to see their "roots." Be sure to include a paragraph on your family's faith tradition. If various branches of your family hail from different traditions, you could include a "faith tree" along with the more traditional geneological tree to show the religious connections of various family members. A faith tree for my family would include my Swedish grandfather, baptized a Lutheran; my Irish-American grandfather, an Anglican; my maternal grandmother, a Byzantine Catholic; my paternal grandmother, raised a Methodist and later an Episcopalian; and my brother, a Southern Baptist. Follow my family ties further

Children are a heritage from God, and the fruit of the womb is a gift.

Psalm 127:4
(*The Saint Helena Breviary, Monastic Edition*)

and you'll find Presbyterians, Roman Catholics and more—many branches intertwined and rooted within Christianity.

Journal about your spirituality. Include more than the weights and heights, lists of visitors, vaccination schedules and developmental milestones of a typical baby book. Talk about your feelings approaching parenthood, your prayers for the new baby, his or her entry into the "household of God" at your church. Think about the miracle of birth and the wonders of seeing a child of God emerge and grow.

Your life is never the same after you become a parent. Think about it, write about it—and give thanks to God.

Gracious Lord,

Thank you for the gift of life.

Thank you for bringing this beautiful child into our home.

As the miracle of our life together unfolds, help me to record faithfully the many milestones along the way. Help me to see your hand at work, guiding me as I guide this child into discipleship. And aid me in telling this story, in pictures and words, to share with my child in the years to come.

Amen.

Grant, O Lord, that all who are baptized into the death of Jesus Christ your Son may live in the power of his resurrection and look for him to come again in glory.

THE BOOK OF COMMON PRAYER, 306

CHAPTER 7

TEACHING TOOLS

Train children in the right way,
and when old, they will not stray.

—Prov 22:6

*M*any parents begin scrapbooks as a family album or an album for a child, chronicling special family events and day-to-day activities. But parents also can use scrapbooks as a teaching tool, either preparing albums to teach their children about God and the church or assembling books with their children to record and support their spiritual growth.

An ABC Spiritual Scrapbook

For the littlest ones, scrapbook lessons can be as simple as A, B, C. Many parents already create small alphabetical albums for or with their children, placing a letter on each page along with appropriate words and photographs to illustrate it. A spiritual scrapbook takes this one step further by adding letter-appropriate spiritual themes.

Upstate New York mother Darcy Fesmire adopted this technique for her children, selecting a Bible verse for each letter. "The Earth is the Lord's and everything in it" illustrated letter E. Letter Y featured "My yoke is easy, and my burden is light." The verses accompanied photos of various letter-specific subjects (brothers reading books for B; cow costume and Caleb's cake for C; Jesus as portrayed in a religious play for J) and lists of other words starting with that letter, biblical and otherwise (for example, hands, hugs, hamburger, helmet and heaven for H).

Variations

Besides letters, a teaching scrapbook easily can combine lessons on colors, seasons and shapes with lessons about God, Bible stories or Scripture verses. Try finding a biblical character or story for each letter. Or work non-alphabetically. Instead of using the ABCs for inspiration, use family and nature photos to illustrate the wonders of God's work in the world, adding your own thoughts or appropriate Bible verses.

A Church Year Scrapbook

Consider organizing an album to follow the church calendar, illustrating it with photos and information about church events throughout the year. My first scrapbook included photos of our family celebrating Shrove Tuesday, Palm Sunday, Holy Week, Easter and Christmas. A teaching album could include those photos and others with explanations of the seasons and holydays of the church year and the Scriptures they are keyed to.

Try using a picture of your child's baptism to illustrate Jesus' baptism as part of the Epiphany season. What about a photo showing lit candles in your

Hear, my child, your father's instruction, and do not reject your mother's teaching.

PROVERBS 1:8

church sanctuary, or showing your toddler gazing raptly at a candle in your home, along with a description of Candlemas, the celebration recalling Jesus' presentation in the temple and recognition by the aged Simeon as the promised Savior who would be a light to the whole world? A closeup of a flower or pictures of your youngster digging in the garden could accompany an entry on the Rogation Days, when farmers' fields traditionally were blessed in the spring. Provide an explanation of All Saints' and All Souls' days along with photos of your family's All Hallows' Eve celebration on October 31.

Such a book could be a learning experience for you as well as your child as you investigate the more obscure celebrations of the church year. You also could include various saints and their symbols (keys for St. Peter, a lamb for St. Agnes). Older children could help with the research or locate appropriate photos and illustrations for each day or saint.

A Spiritual Event Album

With guidance, even younger children can create scrapbook mementoes of spiritually significant events in their lives, such as baptism, Confirmation or a mission trip. Georgia scrapbook consultant Suzanne Ross assembled a small album commemorating her daughter's First Communion. But she also worked with the second-graders in her daughter's Communion class to create "photo-sharing cards" of the event. Marketed by Creative Memories, these are folding cards with clear, photo-mounting sleeves. The children inserted photos, decorated the cards with stickers and added their own comments, including their feelings about the big day. They then could mail the cards to relatives, perhaps a grandparent who couldn't attend the service, or could keep them as mementoes. While not a full-fledged "scrapbook," these cards use the same techniques

For two years, I would get phone calls from mothers saying, "We have to read that almost every single night."

Maurica French

and serve the same purpose as a larger album and are an easy introduction to spiritual scrapbooking for children.

Church school teachers could do similar photo cards or small albums as a class project, perhaps around an event such as the Christmas pageant or a church outreach activity the children participate in. With a little help, primary-school children can attach photos, add stickers and write about what participating in church events means to them. At home, parents and children could assemble an album together, each adding their own reflections on the significance of a religious event or activity.

Preserving Ministry Memories

Scrapbooks can preserve ministry memories for young children that they otherwise would forget. When they lived in the inner city of Orlando, Florida, Maurica French's husband worked for InterVarsity Christian Fellowship and ran urban programs for college students during the summers. The students volunteered at various sites in the area: running camps for children, painting, setting up classrooms.

One summer, Maurica and her young children participated by running a Vacation Bible School-style program with several other mothers and their children at a local rescue shelter for homeless families. At the beginning of the three-week program, Maurica gave each family running the program a disposable camera. At the end, she gave each a small scrapbook, urging the families to record the stories of their experiences. The resulting albums were not the prettiest scrapbooks, Maurica says, but they were the most meaningful she's ever used in ministry.

"For two years, I would get phone calls from mothers saying, 'We have to read that almost every single night,'" she says. "Most of the kids were too little to even remember that event if they hadn't taken that home with them."

Those simple scrapbooks remind these children of the importance of mission—and that they have been co-ministers in such work from their earliest years.

An Album Chronicling Spiritual Growth and Maturity

Older children benefit from album-making, too. In Cranbrook, Michigan, Debby Ball coordinated a scrapbook project that chronologically recorded the events and ministries of young people at Christ Church over seven years through the Journey to Adulthood program, a Christian formation curriculum that guides youngsters from age eleven through eighteen. Participants do service projects, go on a pilgrimage and examine issues of self, society, sexuality and spirituality in the light of the gospel. Christ Church's scrapbooks— four 12- by 15-inch albums—show young people performing service projects, participating in mission trips, enjoying social outings and field trips, assisting with Vacation Bible School, participating in special religious ceremonies, making prayer beads and praying together. Building a community and a sense of shared memories are important aspects of the formation program, says Debby. The scrapbooks fostered that, letting youngsters look back and reminisce about their shared experience and about who they had become through their journey. The pages showed how they grew in leadership, moving from participating in service projects to running them.

The adult advisers assembled the books. "There was a very strong spiritual dimension for us as we were going through it," Debby recalls. "When you go back and look at these memories together, you remember the individual young people you've worked with and some of the spiritual issues they might have been facing at the time. Then you look at where they are now, look at how much has changed."

Some youngsters moved from being less familiar with the spiritual side of their lives to becoming stronger in faith. Some chose to be baptized. Scrapbooks can capture stories of such growth.

The young people provided some journal entries for the albums. That's one change Debby plans if she undertakes another such project: Have the youngsters write more for the albums throughout the process to chronicle their spiritual journey to adulthood.

Confirmation classes and other youth religious-education programs can create similar scrapbooks, with young people writing about and photographing their experiences. They even could assemble the book themselves, either as a one-time event or an ongoing project.

Getting Started

Keep it simple. Don't get bogged down in fancy page decorations. A few stickers and perhaps some simple paper borders are enough. Young scrapbookers may become frustrated or distracted if the process takes too long or involves too much embellishment. And busy parents don't want to take so long working on a teaching album that their children are grown before it's finished! The stories, photos and memorabilia are what's important.

It created a real sense of bonding among the students.

Debby Ball

*Come, O children,
listen to me;
I will teach you
the fear of the Lord.*

Consider whether you want the album to have a uniform look. You can use stickers or a computer to create coordinating titles. Using similar colors or page decorations such as matching banners also works.

Establish a simple system for collecting and organizing photos, journal entries and memorabilia. If creating a scrapbook with young people, consider distributing paper journaling boxes, so they can jot down their thoughts right after an event. Don't forget to gather mementoes such as leaflets from special religious ceremonies, certificates of appreciation from recipients of service projects or brochures from pilgrimage destinations.

Decide whether this is a one-time project or an ongoing commitment. Are you "scrapping" one church event, such as a pilgrimage, where all the youngsters can get together to assemble the album? Or do you want to form a small committee to collect photos and reflections and gather periodically to put them in a scrapbook? For a family album, are you highlighting one religious event, such as baptism, or are you creating a chronological scrapbook of spiritual milestones?

Spread the good news. Don't just display the finished album at youth group meetings. Put it out at coffee hour or your annual ministry fair to show the rest of the congregation what its young people are doing. You might even recruit new youth members or adult advisers!

Above all, find a way to make creating and viewing the scrapbook fun. Remember, we learn best by doing—and the best teachers always seem to make learning fun. That works for spiritual lessons, too.

Teaching scrapbooks can instruct children about their faith, familiarize them with important Scripture verses and with the church seasons, feast days and commemorations, and honor their spiritual milestones. Participating in creating these albums, in a family or a church setting, gives youngsters a chance to reflect on their own spiritual growth, explore the history of their church and ponder what's most important to them about their faith. It's also a fun way to build community, working together on a project stemming from the scrappers' shared faith.

For Reflection and Journaling

- What lessons do you want to teach your child/this group of children?

- How will you organize it: Alphabetically? By church season? Chronologically? By religious milestones?

- What special blessings should be highlighted in this album?

- What do the events depicted in these pages reveal about God and your relationship with the Almighty?

- How can everyone participate and have fun with this project?

All-knowing God, source of all wisdom,

You gave us senses to discover our world and brains to ponder what we find.

Grant us a spirit of exploration and a love of learning. Whether we're reviewing the pages of this album or creating new ones, infuse our time together with a sense of fun and enjoyment of one another's company. Help us to learn your story and recognize your hand at work in our lives, and to share that story with others through this scrapbook.

Amen.

CHAPTER 8

IN LOVING MEMORY

But these also were godly men, whose
righteous deeds have not been forgotten.

—Sir 44:10

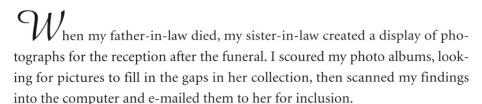

*W*hen my father-in-law died, my sister-in-law created a display of photographs for the reception after the funeral. I scoured my photo albums, looking for pictures to fill in the gaps in her collection, then scanned my findings into the computer and e-mailed them to her for inclusion.

The resulting display showed my father-in-law throughout his life: in childhood, in the Navy, as a newlywed, as a young father, as Pop-Pop and Grandpa. My sister-in-law captioned the photos, so guests could identify years, individuals and locales. For some mourners, the pictures sparked reminiscences. For others, it provided the first glimpse of relatives or friends they had heard stories about or their first information about a passion of Walt's or a family vacation he enjoyed.

I don't know what happened to the display afterward. But for most of those who attended, that was their last look at those pictures, a fleeting glimpse of the life of a man they loved and admired. My originals wait in a stack for reinsertion into my photo albums. I imagine the same thing happens after many funerals: Photographs and memorabilia are displayed for mourners and then whisked away to storage or distribution among family members.

Those pictures and memories don't have to disappear from view. A memorial scrapbook can preserve the story of a loved one's life and survivors' reflections on what that life meant to them. The advent of digital photos and scanning equipment means you don't even need the original photos or documents to create such a book. You can print copies—even multiple copies, if the family wants to assemble duplicate books for several members.

A memorial book is a treasure trove of information and memories about a loved one. Rather than letting family pictures disappear after the funeral, you can do what Patrice Kealy did. After her mother's funeral, she copied all of the pictures the family had displayed and used them to create a "celebration album" of her mother's life. Similarly, she is considering creating a scrapbook of her grandmother's life after hearing family stories at her grandmother's funeral.

"My grandmother had a really hard life and was very bitter about what happened to her," Patrice says. The stories she told her grandchildren focused on the worst times in her life and provided few other details. At the funeral, Patrice and her siblings scrambled to take notes on the background they hadn't heard before. Armed with this information, they visited the Ellis Island website, trying to piece together more details of her life. In her grandmother's belongings, they discovered letters written by her son-in-law, Patrice's father, that she had kept—revealing a hidden sweetness underlying the rockiness of the relationship the two had throughout his marriage to Patrice's mother. A memorial scrapbook for her grandmother would be a "hope album," Patrice says, reveal-

"Do not let your hearts be troubled."

JOHN 14:1

ing a fuller picture of her life and showing "those better things she didn't let most people see."

Sometimes, a scrapbook can reveal such hidden depths. Other times, it introduces a blood relative you've never met. Matt O'Keeffe, who lives in my township, started gathering materials for a memorial scrapbook about his wife after he realized his grandchildren never would know their grandmother. True, his sons told them stories about their grandmother. But Matt wanted to provide as complete a record of her life as possible and his own perspective on the wonderful woman Carol Ann was.

The two met in high school, married while he was in the service and remained wed thirty-two years until she died of brain cancer at age fifty-one in 1992. The church was an integral part of their lives. When they decided to move from New York to New Jersey, they didn't begin looking at houses in a town until they attended worship at the local church to see how they liked the parish. When their priest visited one day during Carol Ann's final illness, they renewed their wedding vows at their home. Her last meal was Holy Communion, administered by friends who were lay ministers. Matt also recalls a funny story about how the church almost ended their relationship, when a teen-aged Carol Ann returned from a church retreat and told him they couldn't date anymore. Back in the 1950s, church leaders apparently considered "going steady" too likely to lead to sins of the flesh. Matt was sure a breakup wasn't necessary, but it took awhile to convince her.

Because the church was so important to them, Matt's scrapbook will include stories about their faith as well as the other events of their life. He's working hard to recover photographs from her early years to supplement the pictures he has from later, but he's also determined to include as many details as possible.

"I'm getting close to the end of my road," he explains. "There's things . . . if I don't put them down, nobody's going to know them."

Ministry to the Dying

When a loved one is terminally ill, scrapbooking can foster healing, deepen faith and preserve family memories. Patrice Kealy's sister helped family members around the country compile an album when their mother was battling cancer, a gift their mother treasured as a source of strength and remembrance when she entered the hospital during the illness that ultimately took her life. Inspired by this, Patrice hopes to offer a scrapbook ministry at her local hospice.

Creating a scrapbook for someone who is dying, or helping that person assemble an album, can provide a sense of closure and capture family history that otherwise soon would disappear. One way to do this is to bring a photo album for the hospice client to look at, then use a tape recorder to collect the stories those pictures elicit. You also can solicit photos, memorabilia, reminiscences and well-wishes to share with the client. Using Scripture verses or hymn lyrics at the top or bottom of each page can help you organize the album around a theme, such as Jesus' resurrection and promises of new life, or the rhythms of life as described in Ecclesiastes ("For everything there is a season . . .).

Photographs also can help people with dementia recall their past, reconnect with family members and tell their stories. Assembling a scrapbook for an Alzheimer's patient can be a precious ministry. The album can provide a focal point for visits and help maintain family ties.

Dealing with death and disease is never easy. A scrapbook can help shift the focus away from a loved one's illness to the memorabilia in the album and put friends and relatives at ease as they assemble or examine it. Relaxing and sharing memories sparked by the scrapbook photos can, in turn, smooth the way for deeper conversations with the dying person about their shared love and the patient's final wishes. I've often been amazed at the intimacy that develops among scrappers as they work communally on their albums, sharing heartfelt stories with near-strangers. Working on a scrapbook with a dying loved one opens the door to greater intimacy, as you share your stories and celebrate the loving ties that death cannot break.

Matt admits it will be hard to work on parts of the book when the memories flow. "There will be times when I'll look at something and not be able to deal with it."

But he sees the therapeutic value of writing about the past. Matt recalls attending the first of two eight-week bereavement seminars and hearing a woman talk about the healing effects of writing down all her feelings. He thought: What good is that? It's not changing anything. Working on his wife's memorial scrapbook years later, he now understands the healing and release that come from the journaling process.

Such therapeutic journaling is not new. When my grandmother died, my minister gave me a copy of C.S. Lewis' *A Grief Observed*, based on Lewis' writings in the early days after his wife's death. The book pours out all his experiences of grief and his questions and demands of God at that time.

Walking with God during such despairing days can help us grow spiritually. Since his wife's death, Matt says, he is more caring about those outside his family and more open to God's promptings to help others. For Mary Wieland of Youngstown, New York, keeping a journal helped her to survive her youngest son's death, deepened her faith and inspired her to serve her church community in new ways.

"Blessed are those who mourn, for they will be comforted."

Matthew 5:4

Keith was twenty-four, a recently graduated civil engineer, when he died in a car crash on September 24, 1994. Six days later, his mother, Mary, wrote her first entry in a notebook: "God never picks any but the most beautiful flowers."

Mary recorded her decision to place meaningful Bible verses, phrases and poetry in the notebook. She cut items from newspapers and wrote down her memories of her son. Sometimes, she entered an item she found along with her reaction to it, such as when she followed the line "I like to think of moments of quiet reflection as a form of prayer" with the observation, "But where and when can anybody find complete quiet these days?"

"That must have been one of my depressing days," she comments.

Along with her relatives and her church family, that small spiral notebook helped her through the trauma. Every morning, she went to her office space in Keith's bedroom, prayed a short prayer service, then sat and wrote. Often she wrote just a sentence or two, perhaps a prayer request, often a Bible verse. She came to look forward to the ritual. She prepared an accompanying album of mostly photographs, tracing Keith's life from birth.

Continuing for five years, the process transformed her, providing an outlet for her emotions and fostering her faith. Formerly someone who just attended church on Sundays, she joined the choir, became senior warden, took on administrative work at the church, engaged in parish activities. She often rereads her book. Its contents provide inspiring words to include when she faces the difficult task of writing a condolence letter.

A memorial scrapbook essentially combines the elements of Mary's two projects, the notebook and the photograph album. Such a book could, like Mary's, form a private, personal remembrance, a place to work through grief and questions of faith sparked by a loved one's death. If eventually shared with others, such an album may, like Lewis' book, provide a powerful testament to the

Yea, though I walk through the valley of the shadow of death, I will fear no evil; for thou art with me.

PSALM 23
(THE BOOK OF COMMON PRAYER, 476)

bereavement journey we all undertake at some point. Less-private memorial scrapbooks, such as those Patrice and Matt envision, provide a valuable portrait of a person's life and faith to inform and inspire both those who knew the person and those who only meet him or her in the pages of the album. These books, in particular, can benefit from involving various people in creating them, since everyone has particular memories to share that others may not know about.

Scrapbooking Guidelines

Gather photos and memorabilia as soon as possible, even if you don't feel able to deal with them until later. One of my lasting regrets is that I didn't save my husband's grandmother's old photo albums when we helped clean out her apartment after she died. We were relative newlyweds living in cramped quarters, so I was trying to limit how much stuff we took and feeling awkward about the whole process. I sorted through several large photo albums, saving the pictures that interested me, but left the rest behind under the impression my husband didn't want them. He later told me he simply hadn't been able to deal with looking at the pictures and deciding which to take; the grief was too fresh.

So keep the old photographs. Box them up out of sight for a while, if you must, but don't discard photo albums and baptismal certificates and diplomas until you can sort through them comfortably and decide which belong in the memorial scrapbook. If there's a funeral display of pictures, try to get copies. They'll make a good starting place for organizing the album.

Consider organizing chronologically. Many scrapbooks have removable pages, so you can insert additional pages at the appropriate spot if more photographs or documents surface after you've completed part of the album.

Lord, now lettest thou thy servant depart in peace . . .

THE SONG OF SIMEON
(THE BOOK OF COMMON
PRAYER, 66)

Enlist others' help in gathering materials and writing stories to accompany photographs. Even if you assemble the book yourself, talk to others about what you're doing. Speaking with someone else—including someone who didn't know the deceased, and therefore will ask questions others wouldn't think to ask—can spark memories and new insights that wouldn't arise if you just worked in isolation.

Include Bible verses or quotations from other religious writings that comfort or inspire you. Consider using lines from Scripture or from a hymn as an organizing tool—one for each page or section of the album.

Include stories of faith, both the deceased's and your own. Do you feel as though God brought you together with your late spouse? Did your dad experience a miraculous rescue during the war? Was Grandpa a pillar of his church? Did your friend exhibit remarkable grace during her long and debilitating illness? Write down those stories and the ways they influenced you.

Write about your feelings. Ask God questions. Include prayers, perhaps leaving space to describe later how they are answered.

Give yourself time. You don't need to complete the album immediately or all at once. A memorial album provides valuable insight into someone's life, and creating it can be cathartic. But it also can be very hard to look at old pictures and deal with powerful emotions. Be patient with yourself. Assembling a memorial album should be a labor of love, not self-torture.

A memorial scrapbook can be a powerful tool: for healing, for preserving the history of someone's life, for introducing a loved one to future generations. Such an album provides an ongoing witness to how someone changed your life and to his or her unique walk of faith on earth.

He that raised up Jesus from the dead will also give life to your mortal bodies, by his Spirit that dwelleth in us.

THE BOOK OF COMMON PRAYER, 485

For Reflection and Journaling

- What are the significant events in this person's life? What stories should you include?

- What did this person mean to you? What did you share?

- What do you know about this person's faith? How did this person live out his or her faith?

- How did this person influence your spiritual path? Was he or she a model of faithful living for you, or one of your spiritual mentors?

- What lessons have you learned while reflecting on this person's life? As you grieve your loss?

Loving Jesus,

You made friends throughout your earthly life, and loved them deeply. You provided for your beloved mother even from the Cross. You cried at the gravesite of your friend Lazarus. You understand grief.

But you also are the Resurrected One. You showed us the life that leads to renewal and rebirth, and the ties that bind us forever in love.

Comfort me in my grief. Help me to remember with thankfulness the times I shared with _____. Guide me in collecting the stories and photographs and memorabilia to prepare a scrapbook of *his/her* life and faith. Renew in me hope and joy, as I await the day when all will be joined together in your kingdom of everlasting love.

Amen.

CHAPTER 9

WHEN TWO OR THREE ARE GATHERED

*'For where two or three are gathered in my name,
I am there among them.'*

—Matt 18:20

𝓘t's often said we learn by doing. The truth is, we also remember by doing.

This happens in simple ways. Just writing down something I need to do and seeing it in print often helps me remember the task, even if I never look at the list again. Similarly, my husband often will say, "Remind me to . . . " because hearing the words helps him to remember. (It doesn't hurt that now he's also enlisted my help!)

Remembering by doing happens in more profound ways as well. When Christians celebrate Holy Communion or the Lord's Supper or the Eucharist, they retell the story of salvation through Christ. But more than that, they perform an act of remembrance: They ritually gather to eat and drink something reminiscent of the bread and wine of that first Eucharist. In a way, they collectively re-experience the Last Supper, as millions of Christians before them have done since the church's earliest days, in accordance with Jesus' command:

"... the Lord Jesus on the night when he was betrayed took a loaf of bread, and when he had given thanks, he broke it and said, 'This is my body that is for you. Do this in remembrance of me.' In the same way he took the cup also, after supper, saying, 'This cup is the new covenant in my blood. Do this, as often as you drink it, in remembrance of me.' For as often as you eat this bread and drink the cup, you proclaim the Lord's death until he comes" (1 Cor 11:23–26).

Tapping into those collective memories is what religious ritual is all about, says Dr. Brent Plate, an assistant professor of religion and visual arts at Texas Christian University. "Memories are stored in our bodies, and rituals are ways to connect with those memories by our actions."

It's a very biblical concept. The Old Testament contains hundreds of injunctions to remember using the Hebrew word *zakhor*, which also essentially means "to act," Plate explains. So when God tells the Israelites to remember something, he also calls them to actions of remembrance. In Deuteronomy, for example, God commands the Israelites to keep his words in their hearts, recite them to their children and discuss them. "Bind them as a sign on your hand, fix them as an emblem on your forehead, and write them on the doorposts of your house and on your gates" (Deut 6:8–9).

Scrapbooking provides a modern forum for such acts of remembrance. Just as with religious ritual, the scrapbook ritual typically involves people gathering in groups, remembering the past and doing something physical, says Plate, who has studied the phenomenon.

The physical part is vital, he says. "You don't just sit around and think about it. You do something with your body."

So is the communal aspect. While scrappers clearly work on their books alone at home, just as many Christians follow private prayer rituals, gathering

"Do this in remembrance of me."

1 Corinthians 11:24

to work in groups is a major component of scrapbooking today. In fact, it may be a modern, individualistic society's answer to our deep need to gather in a group for activities, theorizes Plate. People share their stories, receive validation for them and connect with others who share their stories as well.

Every scrapbook gathering is different, just as every scrapbook is different, yet the ritual of "crops"—like the ritual of many church services—is much the same. Scrappers use similar techniques and tools to shape photos and decorative papers and mount them in albums with other memorabilia, then write facts and reflections about those items. Meeting in community, friends—some of whom know each other only through scrapping—routinely share stories about their lives and family histories in conversations often sparked by the contents of their photos. Like attending worship, it's a familiar, enjoyable ritual. In other words, participating in a modern crop club is an act of scrapbook liturgy.

While anyone can benefit from this ritual, church-related crop clubs can reap real spiritual benefits. In New Jersey, for example, Terry Ferguson started a monthly scrapbook group at the First Baptist Church in Lopatcong. From the outset, she envisioned the group as both a social group for women in the church and an evangelistic tool.

While she sees the group as a way to spread the gospel, it isn't about proselytizing or Bible thumping. The goal was to invite other women to come and see that "Christians don't bite." The church would provide a safe, welcoming environment for socializing and scrapbooking. Or, as Terry puts it, "You can come, and you don't have people talking about what they did at the bar last night."

The venture worked. Women from within and outside the church began gathering to scrap. One young woman learned about the group while church-

Memories are stored in our bodies, and rituals are ways to connect with those memories by our actions.

BRENT PLATE

shopping and started attending services as well as club meetings. To her, such activities signaled a welcoming church, willing to grow and accommodate different needs for different ages and families. Terry describes how another member hasn't joined the church, but she has found friendship and support from the group's church members in times of difficulty. Some of the women have become friends, getting together outside the church to work on their albums or attend scrapbook events.

Scrapping as Ministry

For many women, launching a scrapbook club or becoming a consultant is a direct response to God's call.

When Marielen Christensen began promoting scrapbooking and launched Keeping Memories Alive, it was very much a church-related endeavor. So were Rhonda Anderson's efforts in spreading the word about album-making and starting Creative Memories. "This is definitely my calling," she says.

Sandra Joseph of Pennsylvania knows how she feels. She describes how she always kept scrapbooks, but she felt a real sense of vocation after she discovered Creative Memories at a country fair in 1996. "I just knew as I saw it on this little table that it was my life's calling."

Sandra began reading everything she could find on scrapbooking, even renting Internet time to visit the few websites then available. She started the Tristate Scrapbook Association in Pennsylvania, Ohio and West Virginia, offering scrapbook conventions and even a scrapbooking cruise. Then she sold her idea to Memories Expo, a national consumer show, and began traveling with the expo, monitoring the industry and finding ways to improve the show, which includes stamping and papercrafts as well as scrapbooking.

In 2003, she began Reminders of Faith, whose goal is "to teach people to scrapbook God's faithfulness in their lives." Sandra's company, co-founded with Kathy Brundage, provides inspiration, how-to information, online discussions, products, scrapbook store listings and other assistance. The goal is not to create beautiful scrapbook pages, Sandra explains, but to tell the stories of God's faithfulness behind the photos in albums. Rather than create a separate faith scrapbook, the idea is to incorporate faith stories in every album.

Not all women called to scrapbook ministry start their own companies, but many become consultants and see their work as God-inspired. Dawn Dowdy of California leads "faithbooking" classes in which she provides starter kits at a discounted price, hoping to give women who otherwise might feel shy about discussing their religious beliefs a tool for witnessing to their faith. In Tennessee, Anna Notation-Rhoades plans to use scrapbooking as an outreach tool after her husband completes seminary and is ordained to the ministry. She wants to start church crop clubs, where nonmembers as well as church members can participate, so members can share their stories and newcomers can learn how Christians act and what they believe by observing and conversing with members. Anna describes it as "a way to do missionary work without being in-your-face about it."

"It's like doing witnessing by example in a lot of ways," she says. "That idea really appealed to me."

Church crop clubs also form to provide fellowship opportunities for parishioners. Patrice Kealy started such a group with the blessing of her pastor at St. Thomas the Apostle Catholic Church in Hainesville, New Jersey. She runs the twice-monthly meetings like regular Creative Memories workshops. For each crop, a member acts as workshop "hostess"—personally inviting scrappers and providing refreshments—and Patrice provides scrapbook lessons, advice and supplies. Participants give a donation in lieu of a workshop attendance fee,

You can come, and you don't have people talking about what they did at the bar last night.

TERRY FERGUSON

which the group in turn donates to support the church's youth ministries. Patrice also tithes her proceeds from any product sales to the church.

The group provides important fellowship time for women in the congregation as well as attracts newcomers from outside the church. "People come to know one another in a very personal way," Patrice says.

Participants also strengthen family ties as they work on family albums. One woman created a scrapbook for her beloved grandmother, who was approaching her eightieth birthday. The album-maker later died in a car accident. Patrice muses on what a blessing it was that she took the time to assemble the album for the birthday celebration, strengthening the special connection she had with her family, who now can cherish that keepsake album as a tribute to her. Patrice regularly reports stories like this from the scrapbook club to her pastor. "I keep letting him know the little miracles that happen."

Even when a secular scrapbooking group meets at a church, the environment seems to exert a holy influence. Sandy Schwalb gathers with other consultants at her church in East Tennessee to scrap and exchange ideas—not to mention snacks and recipes. Meeting in a home just isn't the same, she says. "It just gives you that good feeling to have it at a church."

Scrapbook Club Guidelines

Who can join? Is this a group for church members only? Is it a church-sponsored group that's also open to the community? Or is this a secular group that simply wants to meet at the church?

What is the group's focus? Is this primarily or exclusively a social activity? Or does it have a spiritual or evangelistic goal?

People come to know one another in a very personal way.

PATRICE KEALY

For a more spiritually oriented group, you might want to open meetings with prayer or offer particular Bible verses or themes for members to reflect on at each meeting. Some church crop clubs focus on creating faith albums. They organize the club as a workshop, with a designated leader guiding members in creating a faith album, or offer "faithbooking" tips at each meeting. Other groups are open to anyone who wants to work on any type of scrapbook.

If you're hoping to interest scrappers in your church, make sure church literature is available. And consider whether you intend to deliver a particular religious message at meetings or whether, like Terry's group, you simply want to offer a social group in a church setting in the hope that this hospitality will attract newcomers or seekers.

How often will you meet? Is this an ongoing club, or a group meeting for a set period of time to work on a particular project? Scrappers might meet to work jointly on a special album, such as a gift scrapbook for a retiring pastor or the church's ongoing history album. Or individuals might meet for a set time to create their own scrapbooks on a particular faith theme, such as the fruits of the Spirit, the Psalms or the Beatitudes.

Will you serve refreshments? Remember that you want to keep food and drink in a separate area from album-making to avoid crumbs and spills on scrapbook pages. If you offer food, will the church pay for it, or will members contribute the cost or the refreshments? Who's in charge of setup and cleanup?

Members of one secular scrapbooking club I've visited offer a meal before each of their monthly crops, which they hold in one another's homes on a rotating basis. Many churches offer a weekly Lenten supper, followed by an educational program. During Lent, why not provide weekly dinners or host a potluck fellowship, followed by scrapbooking?

It just gives you that good feeling to have it at a church.

SANDY SCHWALB

Will scrappers pay to participate? Some crop clubs, such as Terry's and Patrice's, are initiated by a scrapbook consultant. Do group members want to be able to place orders or buy materials from a consultant during meetings? Will members be asked to pay a workshop fee or make a donation to attend? If so, remember to check to see if there are church restrictions on conducting business on church property. And consider donating any fees to church ministries.

How will you publicize your group? Depending on who you want to invite, consider putting up posters in the community and running announcements in the local newspaper as well as advertising meetings in your church newsletter and on the church's website. Gathering two or three scrappers is great. But with a little publicity, you might attract a bigger group for your "scrapbook liturgy."

The ritual of communal scrapbooking has become a meaningful part of many people's lives. Hosting a church crop club provides a chance to make these experiences even more meaningful, creating fellowship among scrappers in a wholesome environment and offering hospitality to community members who may be hungry for God's good news but reluctant to enter a church for a strictly "religious" program. As Patrice says, in these moments, "little miracles" do happen.

Dear God,

    We meet here to work on our scrapbooks and to enjoy each other's companionship. Please bless our group and our projects. Deepen our friendship and our faith in you and one another. And after we depart, keep us safe until we meet here together once more.

        In Jesus' name,

        Amen.

How lovely is your dwelling place, O Lord of hosts!

Psalm 84:1

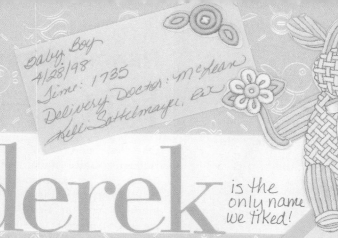
Baby Boy
4/28/98
Time: 1735
Delivery Doctor: McKean
Kelli Sattelmayer, RN

derek
is the only name we liked!

Footprint of Baby

Derek Tyler Dowdy

Born in the Sutter Memorial Hospital of Sacramento, California

On April 28, 1998 at 5:35pm

2 pounds 12 ounces
15½ inches long

```
CH 42378497
DOWDY,DAWN
07/24/68 F029 G026
DR.MENTAKIS,E ALEX   MIP
             04/24/98
```

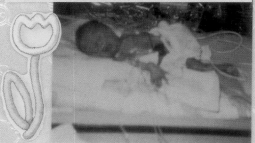

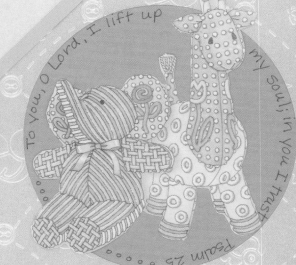

To you, O Lord, I lift up my soul; in you I trust. Psalm 25

REACHING FOR THE
LIGHT

On the occasion of her baptism Katharine Grace Marks took in all the details of her surroundings and the people who were there to witness her initiation into the Body of Christ. Of particular interest to her was the flickering light and glow of the candle on the altar in the chapel. Though she wasn't consciously reaching for the light of Christ, she exhibited that natural tendency in all of us to gravitate toward it. Intuitively, she yearned to be closer to it and be in its presence. In essence, this is precisely what faith is about, the innate desire to be in the presence of God.

At her baptism, Katie's parents, godparents, and those gathered to witness the event made promises to support her in her journey of faith, and in her relationship with God in Christ. Though she could not utter the words for herself, Katie's actions were worth a thousand words, and will serve her well in her journey. God bless you, Katie.

H

happy in a hat

hair * hammer * hand
* happy * harmony *
hats * hearts * heaven
* hellos * helmet * he
home * horses * hugs

1st PLACE

Zach's Facts

- God made you.
- God is always with you.
- God knows what you want or need…even before you ask.
- God understands what it's like to feel sad and alone.

Know that God is the best friend you could ever have!

2005 SUMMER ADVENTURE TREK

PASSPORT

Wild About God

Groups
SERENGETI TREK
Where Kids are WILD about God

NAME Kyler Jorgenson

Celebrate

Clothe yourselves with compassion, kindness,
humility, gentleness and patience.
Bear with each other and forgive whatever grievances
you may have against one another.
Forgive as the Lord forgave you.
And over all these virtues put on love,
which binds them all together in perfect harmony.

Colossians 3:12b-14

seeds of faith

Sometimes you know things before you know that you know them.

This was true for me about a number of things in my faith life. Growing up in the spiritual family of the Society of Friends and the silent form of worship of that body, I experienced aspects of the Christian faith that I didn't know had names until later in life.

I learned about the presence of the Holy Spirit and the communion of that Spirit with the worshiping community that open hearts and transformed lives. I felt the movement and love of that same Spirit when it lifted up the desires and concerns of my own heart as it interceded with "sighs too deep for words."

I learned about the shaping of faith and the gleaning of wisdom as individuals wrestled with, interpreted and shared their life and experiences in worship. Later when I studied the writings and teaching of early church scholars and the lives of spiritual mystics, I came to understand the fullness of what is meant by the communion of saints.

I learned at the feet of modern saints whose lives, individually and corporately, bore witness to the practice of Christian love and charity, and divine justice. Before I could quote scripture, I knew what it meant to live it.

It turns out that my soul is satisfied most deeply by liturgical practices that differ from my religious tradition of origin, but my Quaker roots are deep and continue to nourish me. As my first bishop described me, I'm Quakopalian to the core.

Women
of
Epiphany

Women from the Church of the Epiphany gathered for a weekend retreat at Montgomery Bell State Park in Burns, Tennessee, in March 2000. During that weekend we focused on Benedictine Spirituality, the gifts of silence, prayer, fellowship, work and play, and enjoyed the richness of time together to share our journeys in faith and build deeper relationships.

R Without the usual responsibilities or demands on our time, we were able to slow down and be open to the opportunity for rest and refreshment.

e Sharing our stories and our struggles made it possible to support and encourage each other.

T Our weekend retreat gave us time to enjoy togetherness in a new way.

R A healthy amount of silence allowed us time and space for reflection.

e We had the opportunity to listen to new ideas, consider old ones, contemplate where we were in our journeys, and explore where we felt led to go.

a Our conversations and play time were often animated and full of laughter.

T We enjoyed the freedom to use our time as we chose.

Will and Judy Carter begin a
new life in Christ. This is
what happened to point them
toward their spiritual goal.

august 2001

CHAPTER 10
CELEBRATING SHARED MINISTRIES

For we are God's servants,
working together. . .

—1 Cor 3:9

*T*he urge to preserve memories of times shared with loved ones seems to be universal. Think about how many twenty-fifth-anniversary or fiftieth-birthday celebration planners request old photos and stories to include in a special scrapbook or photo album for the honored couple or individual. I prepared such books for my parents' silver wedding anniversary and my grandparents' golden one. The books were as much fun to assemble as they were for the recipients and their guests to read. I reveled in the pictures that revealed familial resemblances I'd never noticed before; in the formerly unknown tales of youthful hijinks; in the written and photographic testimonies to the power of lifelong friendships.

In a church setting, many congregations create scrapbooks as gifts for departing or retiring ministers. My own parish did this after our last minister

How very good and pleasant it is when kindred live together in unity!

PSALM 133:1

left for a new job in Paris, sending the album with a church member to present to him when he was officially installed in his new post. Such album projects give members a chance to reflect on their church's past and on their relationship with the departing minister. These scrapbooks provide an opportunity for a communal activity, for learning more about their church's history and one another, for reflecting on how they have carried out Christ's work in the world and for closure as they say goodbye to one minister and look toward the ministry of a new one.

As with many things in life, there are easier ways and harder ways to tackle such a project. Deadline pressures make projects more challenging, as longtime scrapper Shannon Jergenson learned when she agreed to create an album for the retiring bishop of the Episcopal Diocese of Olympia, Washington, in only ten days.

Shannon started the album with a handful of photos supplied by her coworkers at the diocesan office, where she is youth program coordinator. But a blanket e-mail to various congregations proved fruitful. Ten pages worth of well-wishes arrived, which she printed and backed with decorative paper. The diocesan communications office and archives provided more old photos and newspaper articles. For a week or more, Shannon was scrapping until 1 a.m., completing about fifty pages for the album. Despite the hard work, Shannon enjoyed the project and gained a new appreciation for the bishop and his ministry.

Creating a scrapbook as a gift is a wonderful way for a church community to commemorate a special occasion. Many people can participate in collecting, organizing and identifying the materials for the album, even if only one person ultimately assembles it. But it's also possible to successfully involve larger

numbers of people in actually creating a scrapbook. New Jersey scrapper
Patrice Kealy used contributed photos and writings to assemble a retirement
album for a priest at her church, then made the scrapbook available to other
parishioners to add their comments and more photos.

A small group also can assemble a gift album—perhaps the church's regular scrapbook club, the committee that maintains the church's history album
or even a group formed for the gift project. At our church, I belonged to a
small committee that planned the scrapbook for our former minister, but we
invited the entire congregation to participate in creating album pages in addition to contributing photos and other memorabilia.

This approach easily can fall into the harder way of doing things. Although
we designated several days for gathering as a congregation to create scrapbook
pages, some people who couldn't attend those workshops assembled their contributions at home with blank pages and photo-safe adhesives we provided.
Some created pages on their computers, and others took home blank pages but
were tardy in returning them—particularly worrisome when the pages were
supposed to highlight specific ministries. An unanticipated problem occurred
when most pages were returned blank on the back, since each family was
allowed a maximum of one side of a page and many people were allotted only
one page side to highlight a particular ministry. We realized partway through
the project that we needed to get something on the back of all those pages before
our deadline—while keeping everything in logical order throughout.

It all worked out fine, of course. We organized the page order, figured out
what should fill in the blanks, then gathered in a small group to fill them in
and finish up. The album looked great, everyone in the parish got to examine
it before it traveled overseas, and the former rector and his wife received their

*They bestowed
many honors on us . . .*

ACTS 28:10

gift enthusiastically. From this experience and others, however, I have learned a few ways to make the process easier.

Scrapbooking Guidelines

Plan ahead. Budget more time than you think it will take. In both Shannon's case and ours, the project grew bigger after we'd already committed to it. People also miss deadlines, so it's best to figure that into the plan.

Look at the materials available, perhaps in your church archives or in files (or boxes) of photos from old bulletin-board displays. Are there particularly meaningful documents or lists you want to include? When the Rev. Anne Fraley received a scrapbook upon leaving a church in St. Louis, she especially appreciated the list of all the people she had baptized, married and buried there. After you know what pictures and documents you have, you can request specific information or photographs to fill historical gaps from the recipient's tenure.

Create a model. Not everyone has seen this sort of scrapbook. Assemble a couple of pages ahead of time as samples for people to look at when they sign up to work on the project or when you solicit photographs and memorabilia.

Provide explicit instructions. Tell people exactly what sort of photos you can use (you may not want printouts on photocopy paper, for example); what sort of adhesives, pens and other materials are photo-safe, if they're creating pages on their own; what size computer-generated pages can be; how many pages (or what portion of a page) contributors can fill; and what the deadlines are for turning in photos and memorabilia or completed pages. If people create pages on their own at home, consider distributing blank pages and strips of photo-safe adhesive along with the instructions. That way, you'll have pages of the right size, free of rubber cement or cellophane tape.

Now, we pray, be with those who leave and with us who stay; and grant that all of us, by drawing ever nearer to you, may always be close to each other in the communion of your saints.

BOOK OF OCCASIONAL SERVICES, 345

Keep page designs simple. When you're assembling a lot of pages in a hurry or involving many people who've never scrapbooked before, it's best not to get too elaborate. Have a supply of basic, photo-safe materials: blank pages, page protectors, black pens, appropriate stickers, photo-cropping tools and some colored paper (perhaps precut). Then have experienced scrappers on hand to walk newcomers through the process of assembling a simple page.

Publicize! Get the word out early and often about materials you're collecting, where to drop them off and what the deadline is. Ditto for pages that contributors assemble at home. And spread the word about scrapbooking get-togethers. Remember not to rely on just one form of communication. Put up posters, print a notice in your parish newsletter, post information on your website, send out a letter (or two), make an announcement on Sunday morning. (This may be tricky if the minister is still there while you're working on the album and you want it to be a surprise. Still, try to spread the word as far and in as many ways as you can.)

Leave room for expansion. Sandy Schwalb's church in Tennessee assembled an album for a departing interim minister, but the congregation also created scrapbook pages of his retirement reception and mailed them to him afterward. We created the scrapbook for our former minister soon after he left, so we already had last-reception photos on hand. But we left blank pages with transparent pockets at the end for him and his wife to slip their own memorabilia into. Patrice's church made the album available for parishioners' additions, even after presenting it to the pastor.

Plan a public viewing of the scrapbook for the entire congregation. It'll give everyone a sense of accomplishment and a unique view of parish life as revealed in the album. Plus, half the fun of scrapbooking is looking at others' pages and showing off your own!

*"This is my
commandment,
that you love
one another as
I have loved you."*

JOHN 15:12

Transitions can be difficult for congregations. It's hard to say good-bye to a beloved pastor, even when members believe the departing minister is accepting a true call and feel excited about the church's new possibilities for mission in the days ahead. Creating a gift scrapbook lets the congregation's members show that minister how much they appreciate him or her. It helps members recognize their minister's spiritual gifts—and their own—and memorialize God's work that they've accomplished together. And it lets church members mourn their loss and bid farewell to one segment of their communal spiritual journey, as they prepare for new beginnings and new ministries.

For Reflection and Journaling

- What are some of the most memorable congregational events of your minister's time there?

- What new ministries began under his or her leadership?

- Who were some of the people most engaged in furthering the church's mission during this time? You might include the names and photographs of staff members, congregational leaders such as deacons, elders or vestry members or lay leaders of particular ministries.

- Do you want to let individual families create pages depicting their special memories of the departing minister?

Liturgy for a Congregation or Church Group Gathering to Create a Gift Scrapbook

Dear God,

We gather today to remember the many gifts and ministries of your servant _____ and to create a scrapbook in *his/her* honor. Help us to remember the blessings we have received; the times we have shared, both good and bad; the good works we have accomplished in your name; and the fellowship we have shared. Inspire our creativity as we assemble the pages of this album. We ask this in your name, creator of all that is good.

Amen.

A Reading from Ecclesiastes

For everything there is a season, and a time for every matter under heaven: a time to be born, and a time to die; a time to plant, and a time to pluck up what is planted; a time to kill, and a time to heal; a time to break down, and a time to build up; a time to weep, and a time to laugh; a time to mourn, and a time to dance; a time to throw away stones, and a time to gather stones together; a time to embrace, and a time to refrain from embracing; a time to seek, and a time to lose; a time to keep, and a time to throw away; a time to tear, and a time to sew; a time to keep silence, and a time to speak; a time to love, and a time to hate; a time for war, and a time for peace.

What gain have the workers from their toil? I have seen the business that God has given to everyone to be busy with. He has made everything suitable for its time; moreover he has put a sense of past and future into their minds, yet they cannot find out what God has done from the beginning to the end.

The word of the Lord.

Thanks be to God.

Remember your leaders, those who spoke the word of God to you; consider the outcome of their way of life, and imitate their faith.

Hebrews 13:7

Let us pray.

> For the ministry of our friend and pastor, _____,
> *We thank you.*
>
> For holy moments and holy laughter, for shared sorrow and shared joy,
> *We thank you.*
>
> As we grieve _____'s departure,
> *Comfort us.*
>
> As we gather to create this special gift,
> *Unite us.*
>
> As we sort our photos and share our memories, decorate our pages
>   and assemble this scrapbook,
> *Inspire us.*
>
> And as we move forward into the next stage of our life together,
> *Guide us.*

Dear Lord,

> You blessed us with _____'s ministry among us and meaningful
> relationships between us. Comfort us now as we mourn *his/her* departure.
> Be with us as we recall the many blessings, special occasions, friendships
> and accomplishments of _____'s time here. Guide our hands as we sort
> and trim photographs, write down our memories and decorate the pages
> of this scrapbook. Let it be a lasting record of our days together and a
> testament to our good wishes. And help us to send forth _____ with
> joy to follow your call.
>
>   In Jesus' name,
>   Amen.

A Prayer of Dedication

Dear God,

In photos and stories, with papers and prayers, we have recorded our loving memories of _____ within the pages of this album. Please bless this scrapbook as we prepare to give it to our friend as *he/she* begins the next phase of *his/her* ministry. Let it ever remind *him/her* of the ministries and friendships we have shared. And please grant to *him/her*, and to us, your wisdom and guidance as we follow our separate vocations in the days ahead.

Amen.

CHAPTER 11
A LASTING WITNESS

'. . . let your light shine before others,
so that they may see your good works
and give glory to your Father in heaven.'

—MATT 5:16

The archives at St. Paul's Cathedral in Buffalo, New York, contain a scrapbook assembled in the 1800s. The album includes letters from the rector at the time, the Rev. William Shelton, who took a grand tour of Europe and the Holy Land while the Episcopal cathedral was being built back home. "He went around visiting all the great cathedrals and different places," recounts cathedral archivist Adrian Cross. "He would send accounts of his journeys back to Buffalo, and they were published in the newspaper and then were snipped and put into a scrapbook."

In one entry, Shelton describes the cathedral in Milan in great detail, comparing it to the structure he hopes is being erected in his absence in Buffalo. In another, posted from Alexandria, Egypt, on April 28, 1865, he writes: "Mr. Editor: I have accomplished the enterprise of travelling through the Holy Land without accident or scarcely a hindrance. I left Bairout on the 5th March and arrived at Joppa (Jaffa) on the 22nd April, having made the entire route on horseback . . .”

The book is old and fragile now, its pages brittle, its covers long gone. But it remains an intriguing window into the cathedral's past, as do donated scrapbooks and photo albums from older parishioners' collections.

Whether created to memorialize a particular event, assembled over time to chronicle a church's ongoing ministry or put together in a one-time history project, scrapbooks can provide an interesting and valuable record of church life. Old photos can document how church buildings and worship styles have changed over time. Pictures and documents can preserve records of staff, former parishioners, bequests and celebrations. They can show a profound truth about how the Holy Spirit has worked through the congregation for many years and provide entertaining revelations about how folks used to dress and style their hair on Sundays.

Scrapbook recollections even can help recreate the past. When the restoration of Shanghai's former Anglican cathedral was planned, officials in China urged Anglicans to search their family albums and church records for early photos and drawings of the building to aid the project. The cathedral was built in 1869 but closed in 1949 after the Communists won the Chinese Civil War.[4]

Sometimes a particular church event launches a historical scrapbook, which then may continue as an ongoing project. When Beverly Pfau joined the women's group at Wharton United Presbyterian Church in New Jersey, she offered to create a scrapbook. The congregation was approaching its centennial, so she began by chronicling the church's history, concentrating on the women's group.

The title page lists the dates: 1901–2001. The album includes an old view of the original Luxemburg Presbyterian Church “from North Main Street by the dam at Washington Pond” and a worship-bulletin cover from 1930 listing Dean

We give thee thanks for the fellowship of those who have worshipped in this place.

THE BOOK OF COMMON PRAYER, 204

A. Dobson Jr., student pastor. There's a history of the Presbyterian Women (originally the Ladies Aid Society), including such intriguing details as: "In 1973, bothered by Madeline Murray O'Hare's protests regarding Bible reading by the astronauts, UPW wrote a letter to NASA supporting them." Several pages describe the church's Holy Rollers, a monthly fund-raising project in which members make hundreds of dinner-plate-sized pasties, or potato pies, so popular there's a waiting list to buy them. There are Ladies Aid Society photos from the 1940s and succeeding decades, pictures of a member's ninetieth-birthday celebration in 2000 and photos and newspaper clippings from the centennial pig roast.

But the book didn't end with the 2001 celebration. Beverly has continued to maintain the album for the women's group, adding photos of activities and special occasions.

At the Church of the Good Samaritan in Knoxville, Tennessee, Sandy Schwalb regularly gathers with other scrappers in her home or at the church to work on the congregation's album. This ongoing project chronicles the church's activities, from youth rafting trips to Vacation Bible School to the annual picnic. When we spoke, Sandy was preparing to track down photos from a wedding reception at the church for a young man the congregation was sponsoring for seminary.

That church album was nearly full, and Sandy already was planning the next one. She's found the scrapbooks serve several purposes.

"We have coffee hour after church, and people love to look at these pictures and look at our albums," she says. They're a good tool to show newcomers the sort of activities the church engages in and to keep current members updated and enthusiastic about church events.

Remember your congregation, which you acquired long ago, which you redeemed to be the tribe of your heritage.

PSALM 74:2

Scrapbooks in Ministry

Faith albums can be a great way to chronicle ministries your church group or congregation participates in, to bear witness to the work you do, to educate others and to interest them in participating in ministries at your church or elsewhere. Sometimes, these scrapbook ministries yield unexpected results.

At her church, scrapbook consultant Anne Lemay regularly displays album pages showcasing the congregation's ministry to seafarers from around the world through the Seamen's Church Institute of New York and New Jersey, an ecumenical agency affiliated with the Episcopal Church that serves and advocates for merchant mariners. A church deacon, Anne has involved members of her former and current New Jersey parishes in providing social and cultural events for seafarers. Anne's scrapbook pages of those events show parishioners what the church is doing and interest them in becoming involved. "The pictures are a form of ministry," she says, "and people will stop and look at them."

Anne's albums also help her minister to the seamen. She brings the scrapbooks to the International Seafarers' Center in Port Newark for the mariners to see. Most seafarers come from other countries, and security restrictions sometimes prevent them from traveling outside the port. Through the albums, however, they learn something about life in America. They also see photographs of other mariners engaging in activities with American volunteers.

The results can be surprising. Thousands of ships pass through the port each year, and while the center staff may see repeat visitors, the church volunteers rarely see the same mariners twice. But one summer, Anne and her husband invited some mariners to their old-fashioned July 4 party. On one table, they displayed her scrapbook album showing pictures of the previous year's party. Some of the seafarers were excited to discover they knew one of the mariners who attended the earlier celebration.

Without the scrapbook, Anne and her guests never would have known about the seafarers' connection with her previous visitor. It served as a reminder of how small the world can be, and of the ties that bind us all throughout God's creation.

In Morristown, Tennessee, Mary Rohe brings the All Saints' Episcopal Church scrapbooks when she visits shut-ins to help them stay connected to the parish. The elderly shut-ins, in turn, provide new details and anecdotes that she incorporates into the church's growing album collection. Shepherding the church's scrapbook project has been Mary's ministry since she retired from nursing in 1999. In six years, All Saints' scrappers completed ten albums tracing the church's history since 1940. Mary has assembled additional albums to record special church events, such as a choir trip to perform at the National Cathedral in Washington, D.C., and created scrapbooks documenting several years in the life of the Diocese of Tennessee and of the parish's school.

Without such albums on hand, details of a church's history can disappear quickly. I attend church in a transient area, filled with large corporations that routinely transfer families in and out of New Jersey. Some companies have cut their workforces dramatically, forcing some former employees to relocate in search of new jobs or careers. Although the twenty years I've spent in our parish generally don't feel like a long time to me, I can count many people who have come and gone during those years. The church staff has turned over completely, with some jobs changing personnel several times and several positions added or reconfigured. We've conducted two capital campaigns—renovating the church, parish hall, rectory, onsite child-care center, church school, gardens, organ and carillon—and bought and sold housing for our associate

The pictures are a form of ministry, and people will stop and look at them.

Anne Lemay

clergy. We've revamped our outreach organization, expanded our church school and youth programs, sent choirs on tour and entered companionship relationships involving exchange trips, prayer support and overseas ministries, first with a church in South Africa and later with a group of congregations in South India.

In short, a lot has happened during those two decades, and many, many newcomers arrive unaware of that history. One of our parishioners recently updated a book about the history of our church. But photographs and actual documents are scattered. When we assembled a few pages of church history for the gift album for our former minister, it was hard even to gather photos of all of the staff who had served during his tenure, let alone all the parish events during that time—and that was only six and a half years.

This then is the challenge and the value of church history projects.

The challenge is finding pictures and documents from the congregation's past. It takes time and persistence. Even when parishioners photograph events and display the pictures on bulletin boards, those photos may disappear afterward. Old service leaflets, newspaper clippings and meeting minutes wind up in boxes—or even thrown away.

The value, of course, is preserving that church history in words and photographs for current and future generations to show how the community has spread the gospel by worshipping together and caring for one another and the community. Once captured in a scrapbook, the record remains—and all in one place.

Churches create history albums in different ways. A church could assemble an album chronicling a particular period of its history, such as the Wharton album, which began as a centennial remembrance. A church can record

"Go therefore and make disciples of all nations . . ."

Matthew 28:19

[W]e will tell to the coming generation the glorious deeds of the Lord, and his might, and the wonders that he has done.

Psalm 78:4

history as it happens, starting with current photos. Or a church might catalogue its past and then continue adding current events. Either a group or an individual may assemble and maintain a church album.

A few general guidelines can help produce any of these variations.

Don't rush the project. Give yourself—and fellow church members—time to gather photos, locate newspaper articles and remember old stories.

Get organized. Create a central location for people to drop off photographs or other contributions—perhaps a box or folder in the church office or lobby. Encourage contributors to select their best pictures for possible inclusion, rather than hand the committee a computer disc of three hundred digital photos of a church event to sort through. Catalogue materials as they come in, grouping items chronologically or by topic (youth group photos in one envelope, parish suppers in another).

Preserve the materials. Placing items in archival-quality albums using photo-safe products helps preserve historical photos and documents. When members want their photographs returned, the church prefers to keep original documents in its archives or a newspaper clipping is yellowed and disintegrating, take advantage of scanners and computers to copy the materials, enlarging or enhancing them if necessary. Be sure to use photo-safe paper for copying paper documents and to print photographs onto photo paper, a process that may require a specific type of printer.

Collect people's reminiscences. Names and dates are important, but the really fun part of family histories—including church-family histories—is the stories. The Episcopal church where I grew up, for example, dates from pre-Revolutionary War days and contains bullet holes in the steeple from a Revolutionary War battle on the nearby green. We were the Tory church, the

Presbyterians beside us the revolutionary Whigs, and the battle was halted by a sudden thunderstorm. It's also interesting to ponder the slave gallery upstairs, with its pew backs uncomfortably slanted forward, and how the existence of slavery meshed with Christian teaching at the time.

At my current church, we like to talk about how Hetty Green, a wealthy but miserly businesswoman, had her daughter, Sylvia, married at our parish to save money. Neither she nor her daughter was a member. But when Sylvia Wilks died in 1951, she left a considerable sum of her inheritance to the church, creating a multimillion-dollar endowment the congregation has used ever since, mostly for outreach ministries. As a newspaper reporter, I once heard this story repeated during a secular walking tour of the town. That's the sort of story to include in a parish scrapbook.

An album can include less dramatic stories as well. A photo of my church's bell tower, for example, might include details about the bells and where they were made; the fact that the tower is the tallest point in town; and a description of how for years the girls' choir annually trekked the long, spiral staircase to the tower's top as part of a church tour.

History isn't just the far past. It happens as we make it, and things often change faster than we realize at the time. A church's members, leaders, ministries, architecture, size, location and denominational affiliation all affect its mission, and those things may change through the years. A church album helps capture that history before it's forgotten and reminds members of the roots of their congregation's faith. It shows how faithful members have lived out the gospel over time—in different ways, perhaps, but always seeking to follow God's call. And it provides perspective and inspiration for the members of today and in the years to come.

We give thanks to you, O Lord our God, for all your servants and witnesses of time past . . .

THE BOOK OF COMMON PRAYER, 838

For Reflection and Journaling

- What do you know about your church's founding and when it was built?

- What events and ministries have shaped your congregational life?

- How has your congregation demonstrated God's love to its members and its neighbors? How has it spread the gospel to the world?

- Which members, clergy and other staff have played key roles in your church's history?

- Do you want to include lists: for example, of those baptized or confirmed at the church; of those buried in the church graveyard or memorial garden; of church leaders and when they served; of church committees and their members; of important dates in your church's history; of bequests?

God of our ancestors,

You remember the good deeds of the saints of every age. Bless the work of this committee, as we fashion a lasting record of the ministries of this congregation in your service. Help us faithfully to chronicle the names, dates, events and stories of this church's work within our community and the wider world as we seek to spread your good news. Let this scrapbook be our witness and inspiration to the generations to come.

Amen.

CHAPTER 12
TOOLS OF THE TRADE

By wisdom a house is built, and
by understanding it is established.

—Prov 24:3

*S*crapbooking sounds simple. Glue a few photos in a book, write down some details and reminiscences—how hard can it be?

On the other hand, if you've ever ventured into a large craft or scrapbook store, or browsed through a highly decorated album, you may feel intimidated by how complicated it all looks. Decorative scissors, innumerable stickers, fancy papers, cutting tools, die cuts, pens, page covers, embossing kits—who has the time and money to master it all?

The answer lies somewhere in between. You can create a simple and meaningful scrapbook with a handful of photos and memorabilia and a photo-safe album, adhesive and pen. For a few more dollars, you can crop photos quickly and easily, add colorful and decorative accents to your pages and organize your materials using some of the specialized tools on the market. The goal of a faith album is to tell your faith story, not to turn out the most intricately decorated and showy scrapbook pages possible. Still, it's fun to use some of the scrapbook tools and to use your creativity to enhance the album and create a cohesive look for your pages. How much you tend toward the simple or the complex is up to you.

Photo-Safe Materials

When choosing scrapbook products, look for items that are photo-safe, fast and fun. Most important is using photo-safe albums and other materials. At my first scrapbook workshop, my friend and consultant Tracy Bridges showed a ten-year-old album containing some of her wedding photos. Already, the pages and photos were yellowing—something that wouldn't happen in an album with acid-free, lignin-free pages, which protect photographs and keep pages from turning brown. Buffered album pages have a protective coating to keep the photo-damaging chemicals in anything acidic you mount on them— say a concert ticket or worship bulletin—from spreading to the pictures elsewhere on the page, providing another line of defense against photo damage.

You don't want to go through all the effort of constructing albums only to have them disintegrate or the photographs fade. So be very careful which scrapbook materials you use. Although many archival-quality products are on the market, industry standards addressing what terms like "photo-safe" mean are only voluntary. Just because a sticker or pack of paper is labeled "acid-free" doesn't mean that it actually is. As Rhonda Anderson puts it, "There's no archival police."

When searching for photo-safe materials, look for products made by reputable companies. Ask other scrappers what materials they use and how they've

[K]eep sound wisdom and prudence . . .

PROVERBS 3:21

held up over time. Consider contacting companies to ask what standards they follow and how they determine their products meet those standards. Ph testing kits and "deacidification" products are available, but I can't vouch for their effectiveness. If you're uncertain about the acidity of a particular sticker, decorative paper or piece of memorabilia, mount it so that it doesn't touch any photographs on the album page.

Beyond selecting photo-safe materials, scrappers face a wide array of choices and tools. This is where "fast and fun" fit in.

Albums

In choosing an album, consider the type of faith scrapbook you're making. A small book works well for a gift album—such as the one Patrice Kealy made to describe her faith to her husband—or to record a particular event, such as a baptism, ordination, mission trip or retreat weekend. A large book—say 12 by 15 inches—lends itself to an ongoing church history or ministry book because it can incorporate larger documents and more photos. A 12- by 12-inch album fits on an average bookcase and might be appropriate for a personal faith album, memorial book or wedding album.

Scrapbooks come in several basic constructions. Some albums use plastic straps that thread through the backs of removable pages, which lie flat when opened. Pages in a loose-leaf or spiral-bound book also can lie flat. My baby album uses removable pages mounted on posts that go through reinforced holes, but they don't lie flat easily when you open the book. For this album, I prefer to remove the pages to work on them because it's easier to work on a flat surface. An album bound like a typical hardcover book similarly wouldn't lie flat.

Particularly for a long-term project, or one in which different people will contribute pages, consider a scrapbook with removable pages so you can rearrange pages or insert new ones. Although I organize my books chronologically, I like to work on pages in order of interest, or in the order in which I locate the materials I want to incorporate, and then to rearrange the book as I go along, rather than having to decide precisely what goes on each page before I start. For a group project, removable pages mean everyone can work on pages independently, whether at a group "crop" or alone at home, while the scrapbook itself stays in a safe, central location.

Some scrapbooks are "top-loading." They contain a plastic sleeve, with scrapbook pages inserted through a hole in the top. You remove the page, decorate it—perhaps covering it over partly or entirely with colored or patterned paper before adding photos and journal entries—then slip it back into its plastic sleeve to protect it. Other albums are composed of thicker blank pages, which you "scrap," then cover with a plastic protective sleeve that you pull over them from the side. It's always a good idea to protect pages from fingerprints and to prevent items from being ripped or pulled off accidentally.

Adhesives

Photo-safe adhesive products include double-sided tape in various forms. Try rolls of tape for long strips of adhesive to mount large pieces of paper, or pre-cut strips of adhesive for small pieces to use on photo corners. Automatic dispensers come in varying tape widths and let you determine how much adhesive to use with each application.

Be sure to choose an adhesive that's strong enough for the job as well as photo-safe. I once heard a scrapper recount how she carefully adhered items to album pages using a glue stick—only to have everything fall off when she lifted the pages to show someone.

Decorative Papers, Pens and More

The seemingly endless array of decorative papers offers a rainbow of colors, patterns from stripes to waves to gingham, inspirational sayings and thematic backgrounds featuring everything from grass to Noah's ark to piano keyboards to fireworks. Papers come in full sheets of various sizes and in precut shapes such as rectangles, triangles and long, thin strips. Other decorative items include die-cut shapes, appliques and stickers for any occasion and interest—birthdays, Bible verses or babies, travel, tennis or Tennessee. Pens come in varying colors and styles, from calligraphic to fine-tip to wide-tip. Some crafters combine hobbies, using rubber-stamp kits to decorate their album pages.

Cutting Tools

While you can mount photos just as they are, or trim them with ordinary scissors, specialized cutting tools can be quicker, neater and fancier. My first and favorite cutting tool is the "personal trimmer," a Creative Memories product that looks like a small paper cutter. It's ideal for trimming photos and papers quickly and neatly, with straight lines. Other cutting tools can round off photo corners; cut pictures or papers into circles, ovals or other shapes; punch out paper designs such as hearts or stars; and trim paper into decorative strips and borders. It's possible, of course, to cut a photo into a circle without one of these tools. If you're like me, however, you'll have a harder

There's no archival police.

Rhonda Anderson

time and take longer cutting a perfect circle freehand or using a stencil than if you use one of these specialized tools. These products are designed to be faster and more accurate. Add in the funky shapes and fancy borders, and you've found the fun as well.

Don't feel as though you need to buy everything at once—or even that you need it all. It's fine to start with a few album pages, a pen and adhesive, then add materials as you go along. Attending workshops or joining a crop club gives you a chance to try out or share tools. Some scrappers also swap papers and stickers.

Using the Computer

Computers are fast becoming valuable tools for scrappers. Although it's important to include your handwriting in an album for posterity—it's a distinctive and treasured characteristic—using a computer for some journaling lets you fit more writing on a page, take time to compose your thoughts, correct typos and print legible stories on various shades of paper. Some album kits are designed specifically to use computer-generated materials. As with your other materials, just be sure the paper is archival-quality. Some companies even let you assemble a scrapbook digitally, then will send you the physical, completed album.

Finally, remember that tools are just that—a way to help you get the job done, not an end in themselves. The goal is to create a meaningful, lasting scrapbook, not to amass the most complete tool collection. For faith scrapbooks in particular, the meaning lies far more in the beauty of the story told than in the beauty of the album pages.

Give us the tools, and we will finish the job.

WINSTON CHURCHILL
(1874–1965)[5]

Strips and scraps and plastic sleeves,
Kaleidoscope colors and memories,
Die cuts and stickers and two-sided tape—
Dear Lord, what a glorious mess it all makes!

But out of these tools and crafter's passion
A powerful album I hope to fashion.
Guide my art as I tell this story
and make this record to your glory.

CHAPTER 13
PAGE DESIGN

'This is how you are to make it . . .'
—GEN 6:15

A few years ago, a friend asked me how I write a poem. Thinking about it, I realized that I nearly always begin with a visual image—a cud-chewing cow, a soldier stationed at Christ's cross, a broken tricycle—and build the poem around it. The cow evokes a gossipy lady, the centurion provides a viewpoint for exploring the Crucifixion, the tricycle symbolizes a child killed by a drunken driver.

Images are powerful. That's the truth behind the saying that "a picture is worth a thousand words." And that's what makes a scrapbook so powerful: The images and the way you present them are as important as—or even more important than—the words that accompany them.

Don't worry if you think you're a poor photographer or are artistically challenged. In this sense, scrapbooking is more like quiltmaking than poetry writing. There are basic techniques and patterns to follow. You can copy others' page designs or borrow page-decorating techniques. Craft stores and consultants offer workshops. Depending on your taste, time constraints and abilities, you can create pages that are simple, complex or somewhere in between. Like a family quilt, even if it follows a particular pattern, each scrapbook is unique because it tells a unique story.

I love designing scrapbook pages just as I loved creating paper "dummies" of newspaper pages and pasting up the strips of typeset copy in the days before everything was designed on computers. Scrapbooking is even better because it lets me tell my own story—without having to design around those pesky ads that help pay my salary!

For those feeling a little less certain about their design capabilities, here are some guidelines.

First, choose your photos. Toss aside the blurry pictures, the unflattering images and the near-duplicates. Don't worry if you only like part of a picture, however; that's what cropping's for.

Group the photos that will go on a page or pages. If you're chronicling a baptism or baby dedication, for example, you might fill several pages. Perhaps the first page will show pre-service family photos, the second page the service itself and photos of the godparents and clergy with the baby and the third page pictures from the celebration afterwards. While it varies from page to page and scrapper to scrapper, four to six photos usually is a good number for a 12-inch by 12-inch scrapbook page. Don't worry if they don't all fit in their original size—again, cropping can resolve this.

Next, crop the photos. Don't feel obligated to cut a photograph you think is perfect. But many pictures benefit from at least a little trimming. Cut out unnecessary or distracting backgrounds—endless lawn stretching before the feet of your subjects, extraneous clutter on the table beside them, the back of someone's head. Some photos may lend themselves to being cut into a shape, such as a circle or oval. Occasionally, you may wish to use scissors to cut along the outline of a subject to lift it completely out of the background.

I've always been a picture person. If I read a book, I want to see a picture. That's why I'm so into scrapbooking. I want more than just the words.

Marielen Christensen

You can tell people as much as you want, but to actually see it is a whole different story.

Shannon Jergenson

Now, you're ready to design the page. In newspaper design, the goal is to guide the reader through each page, presenting the most important information in the most prominent places and with the biggest headlines. Thus the most important articles appear at the top of the page, less-important ones sequentially lower down. Photos also call more or less attention to themselves, depending on their size, shape and placement. A well-designed scrapbook page similarly shows the viewer where to look first. The title—your main headline, if you will—should be in bigger letters than the photo descriptions and other journaling. The biggest and best photos should go in the most prominent place on the page.

When possible, avoid using square pictures. Ever notice how the standard photo-printing sizes are rectangular—8 by 10, 5 by 7, 4 by 6? Crop to similar proportions—or even exaggerate the rectangular shape, if a photo lends itself to that.

Vary the sizes of photos on a page. Don't line up three identical-sized pictures beside each other. As on a well-designed newspaper page, using different sizes of photos on a scrapbook page guides the viewer's eye through the material and makes it easy to distinguish one image from another. Of course, there are exceptions. If you're creating a page full of family portraits cut into circles and arranged as Christmas-tree ornaments, for example, you may want to cut the circles the same size. Several shots showing an event sequentially, such as a child coming down a slide into a pool, also might work best if cut the same size.

Place photos logically according to what they depict. If a picture shows someone gazing into the distance to the right, don't place the photo at the outer edge of a right-hand page. Place it so the person is looking into the page—or even toward the subject of another photo on the page. Or, if you're arranging that sequence of the child on the slide, let the series slide down the page vertically or diagonally instead of placing the pictures side-by-side.

While some variety is good, too much breeds chaos. Feature one or two photo shapes on a page, not five. Don't use umpteen fonts for your lettering unless the subject warrants a circus flyer/wanted poster approach. Remember that one or two good-sized photos usually tell a story better than six small ones.

On scrapbook pages, as in life, balance is best. Try not to make the page top-heavy, for example, with several large photos in the upper part of the page and almost nothing on the bottom. When designing two facing pages, look for overall balance across the spread. But don't feel obligated to make pages rigidly symmetrical. A slight asymmetry to the page or using an odd number of photos can enhance its appearance, just as the best photos typically don't pose the main subject precisely front-and-center.

Keep photos visible. If you use patterned paper, be sure the photos don't get lost in the fancy background. Matting photographs on plain-colored paper helps them stand out from the designs on the decorative paper behind them.

Simplify. There's nothing wrong with elaborately decorated pages, but getting too fancy can interfere with your ability to ever finish a project. Try matting one or two photos on a page, placing them on a colored piece of paper just slightly larger than the photo. Even simpler, place a long thin strip of colored paper down the side, along the top of the page or diagonally through the middle to highlight one of the colors in your photos.

Add a shape or two to the background, such as a colored triangle or heart. Display a biblical quotation. Scatter a few stickers across the page. Again, don't overdo it. Include enough decoration to highlight or illustrate your subject, not overwhelm it.

Some people decorate pages ahead of time along certain themes, then add photos later. Some even decorate scrapbooks as gifts—say a baby book for a new mother—leaving the recipients to choose and mount pictures. Others prefer to design pages as they go to suit each set of photos.

Whichever style suits you, pay attention to how you decorate facing pages. It provides a more coherent look to your book if you use similar features on those pages. You might matte photos on both pages using the same background colors or use a strip of same-colored paper on the outside edge of each page. If you're doing several pages on the same theme, consider using similar colors, stickers, lettering or other decorative items throughout those pages. For an entire book on a particular theme—say a wedding or baby album—you might use the same lettering style for section titles.

Most important, of course, is to choose the decorative style that you like best and that will encourage you to keep working on your scrapbook. Remember, this should be fun!

Eternal God,
 You gave birth to the universe and unfolded the patterns of the stars. You painted the wings of the butterflies and the colorful multitudes of the sea. You formed us from the dust of earth into bodies of intricate design, from whirled fingertips to rhythm-beating hearts.
 I long to join in your act of creation.
 Inspire me as I design these pages, choosing the best photographs, colors, stickers and stories. Help me to create a scrapbook that is pleasing to see as well as to read, as I seek to share your story through this album.
 Amen.

CHAPTER 14
WORDS TO SCRAP BY

For whatever was written in former days was written for
our instruction, so that by steadfastness and by the
encouragement of the scriptures we might have hope.

—Rom 15:4

"But I'm not a writer."

I cannot count how many times I've heard people say this or something
like it. Sometimes I parrot what author Madeleine L'Engle said when people at
writers' workshops stated this during their introductions, no doubt meaning
they weren't professional or published writers: "If you write, you're a writer."

Still, I understand how shy people can feel about committing their
thoughts to words if they don't feel skilled at it, much as many a shower-song-
ster refuses to sing in public. And that can prove a barrier in creating a faith
album, or even an ordinary family scrapbook, where the journaling is as valuable as the photos.

As important as the journaling is, however, no law says you can't use others' words to get your point across. Sometimes, the Scriptures say it best, and a
few verses from the Bible provide a compelling message about what you're
feeling or thinking as you create a scrapbook page. Scripture passages also can

provide an organizing theme for your faith album, to inspire and accompany your photos and journal entries.

Creative Memories founder Rhonda Anderson provides a detailed biblical concordance—Scripture references on various topics—through her consultants to scrappers interested in creating faith albums. The scrapbook concordance makes it easy to find suitable Bible verses for all sorts of events and topics, with listings such as "athletics/sports," "courage" and "friends." Under subjects like "babies," the concordance lists biblical passages in numerous subcategories, such as "sleeping," "sonogram" and "visitors."

Other sources of inspiring words abound, starting with the Bible and continuing through prayer books, hymnals, books of quotations, newspaper columns and poetry collections. Look through anthologies of writings and sermons by people who inspire you: C.S. Lewis, Billy Graham, Mother Theresa, Dietrich Bonhoeffer. Examine some of the many collections of prayers, such as *The Oxford Book of Prayer*, *Plain Prayers in a Complicated World* by Avery Brooke, *Prayers from the Heart* by Richard Foster, *An African Prayer Book* by Desmond Tutu, *The Anglican Family Prayer Book* by Anne E. Kitch and *Peace Prayers: Meditations, Affirmations, Invocations, Poems, and Prayers for Peace* edited by the staff of Harper San Francisco, Carrie Leadingham, Joann E. Moschella and Hilary M. Vartanian.

Here's a selection of Bible verses, hymns, prayers, and quotations covering a wide range of circumstances and emotions. You may want to incorporate some of them into your faith album—but don't stop here. I hope this list inspires you to find your own meaningful passages of Scripture, to locate or write your own prayers or poetry and to use your own favorite quotations and hymns to enhance your pages and explain and share your faith through your scrapbook.

Scriptures

Praises

I will give thanks to the Lord with my whole heart; I will tell of all
your wonderful deeds. (Ps 9:1)

Make a joyful noise to God, all the earth; sing the glory of his name.
(Ps 66:1–2)

How lovely is your dwelling place, O Lord of hosts! (Ps 84:1)

"My soul magnifies the Lord, and my spirit rejoices in God my
Savior." (Luke 1:46–47)

Petitions

May God be gracious to us and bless us and make his face to shine
upon us. (Ps 67:1)

Let the words of my mouth and the meditation of my heart be
acceptable to you, O Lord, my rock and my redeemer. (Ps 19:14)

"Pray then in this way:
Our Father in heaven,
hallowed be your name.
Your kingdom come.
Your will be done,
on earth as it is in heaven.

> Give us this day our daily bread.
> And forgive us our debts,
> as we also have forgiven our debtors.
> And do not bring us to the time of trial,
> but rescue us from the evil one." (Matt 6:9–13)

> Ask, and it will be given you; search, and you will find; knock, and the door will be opened for you. (Matt 7:7)

Words of Comfort

> Do not be far from me, for trouble is near and there is no one to help. (Ps 22:11)

> Who will separate us from the love of Christ? Will hardship, or distress, or persecution, or famine, or nakedness, or peril, or the sword? . . . No, in all these things we are more than conquerors through him who loved us. For I am convinced that neither death, nor life, nor angels, nor rulers, nor things present, nor things to come, nor powers, nor height, nor depth, nor anything else in all creation, will be able to separate us from the love of God in Christ Jesus our Lord. (Rom 8:35, 37–39)

> Draw near to God, and he will draw near to you. (Jas 4:8)

> "Therefore I tell you, do not worry about your life, what you will eat or what you will drink, or about your body, what you will wear. Is not life more than food, and the body more than clothing? Look at the

birds of the air; they neither sow nor reap nor gather into barns, and yet your heavenly Father feeds them. Are you not of more value than they? And can any of you by worrying add a single hour to your span of life? And why do you worry about clothing? Consider the lilies of the field, how they grow; they neither toil nor spin, yet I tell you, even Solomon in all his glory was not clothed like one of these. But if God so clothes the grass of the field, which is alive today, and tomorrow is thrown into the oven, will he not much more clothe you—you of little faith? (Matt 6:25–30)

"See, the home of God is among mortals.
He will dwell with them;
they will be his peoples,
and God himself will be with them;
he will wipe every tear from their eyes.
Death will be no more;
mourning and crying and pain will be no more,
for the first things have passed away." (Rev 21:3–4)

Christian Virtues

"Blessed are the poor in spirit, for theirs is the kingdom of heaven.
"Blessed are those who mourn, for they will be comforted.
"Blessed are the meek, for they will inherit the earth.
"Blessed are those who hunger and thirst for righteousness,
    for they will be filled.
"Blessed are the merciful, for they will receive mercy.
"Blessed are the pure in heart, for they will see God.

"Blessed are the peacemakers, for they will be called children of God.
"Blessed are those who are persecuted for righteousness' sake, for
theirs is the kingdom of heaven.
"Blessed are you when people revile you and persecute you and utter
all kinds of evil against you falsely on my account. Rejoice and be
glad, for your reward is great in heaven, for in the same way they
persecuted the prophets who were before you." (Matt 5: 3–13)

Now there are varieties of gifts, but the same Spirit; and there
are varieties of services, but the same Lord; and there are varieties
of activities, but it is the same God who activates all of them in
everyone. To each is given the manifestation of the Spirit for the
common good. To one is given through the Spirit the utterance of
wisdom, and to another the utterance of knowledge according to
the same Spirit, to another faith by the same Spirit, to another gifts
of healing by the one Spirit, to another the working of miracles, to
another prophecy, to another the discernment of spirits, to another
various kinds of tongues, to another the interpretation of tongues.
(1 Cor 12:4–10)

Love is patient; love is kind; love is not envious or boastful or
arrogant or rude. It does not insist on its own way; it is not irritable
or resentful; it does not rejoice in wrongdoing, but rejoices in the
truth. It bears all things, believes all things, hopes all things, endures
all things. Love never ends. (1 Cor 13:4–8)

[T]he fruit of the Spirit is love, joy, peace, patience, kindness,
generosity, faithfulness, gentleness, and self-control. (Gal 5:22–23)

Now faith is the assurance of things hoped for, the conviction of
things not seen. (Heb 11:1)

Serving God

Then I heard the voice of the Lord saying, "Whom shall I send, and
who will go for us?" And I said, "Here am I; send me!" (Isa 6:8)

"In everything, do to others as you would have them do to you."
(Matt 7:12)

"Go therefore and make disciples of all nations, baptizing them in
the name of the Father and of the Son and of the Holy Spirit, and
teaching them to obey everything that I have commanded you. . . .
(Matt 28:19–20)

Devote yourselves to prayer, keeping alert in it with thanksgiving.
(Col 4:2)

But be doers of the word, and not merely hearers . . . (Jas 1:22)

Salvation's Story

The people who walked in darkness have seen a great light . . . For a child has been born for us, a son given to us; authority rests upon his shoulders; and he is named Wonderful Counselor, Mighty God, Everlasting Father, Prince of Peace. (Isa 9:2, 6)

In the beginning was the Word, and the Word was with God, and the Word was God. He was in the beginning with God. All things came into being through him, and without him not one thing came into being. What has come into being in him was life, and the life was the light of all people. The light shines in the darkness, and the darkness did not overcome it. . . . And the Word became flesh and lived among us, and we have seen his glory, the glory as of a father's only son, full of grace and truth. (John 1:1–5, 14)

"For God so loved the world that he gave his only Son, so that everyone who believes in him may not perish but may have eternal life. "Indeed, God did not send the Son into the world to condemn the world, but in order that the world might be saved through him." (John 3:16–17)

. . . "I truly understand that God shows no partiality, but in every nation anyone who fears him and does what is right is acceptable to him." (Acts 10:34–35)

Hymns

All things bright and beautiful

Refrain:

> All things bright and beautiful,
> all creatures great and small,
> all things wise and wonderful,
> the Lord God made them all.

Verses:

> Each little flower that opens,
> each little bird that sings,
> he made their glowing colors,
> he made their tiny wings.

> The purple-headed mountain,
> the river running by,
> the sunset and the morning
> that brightens up the sky.

> The cold wind in the winter,
> the pleasant summer sun,
> the ripe fruits in the garden,
> he made them every one.

> He gave us eyes to see them,
> and lips that we might tell
> how great is God Almighty,
> who has made all things well.

All who believe and are baptized

All who believe and are baptized
shall see the Lord's salvation;
baptized into the death of Christ,
each is a new creation.
Through Christ's redemption we shall stand
among the glorious heavenly band
of every tribe and nation.

With one accord, O God, we pray:
grant us thy Holy Spirit;
help us in our infirmity
through Jesus' blood and merit.
Grant us to grow in grace each day
that as is promised here we may
eternal life inherit.

Day by day

Day by day, dear Lord, of thee three things I pray:
to see thee more clearly, love thee more dearly,
follow thee more nearly, day by day.

He is risen (vs. 1)

He is risen, he is risen!
Tell it out with joyful voice;
he has burst his three days' prison;

let the whole wide earth rejoice:
death is conquered, we are free,
Christ has won the victory.

Joyful, joyful

Joyful, joyful, we adore thee,
God of glory, Lord of love;
hearts unfold like flowers before thee,
praising thee, their sun above.
Melt the clouds of sin and sadness;
drive the dark of doubt away;
giver of immortal gladness,
fill us with the light of day.

All thy works with joy surround thee,
earth and heaven reflect thy rays,
stars and angels sing around thee,
center of unbroken praise.
Field and forest, vale and mountain,
blooming meadow, flashing sea,
chanting bird and flowing fountain,
call us to rejoice in thee.

Thou art giving and forgiving
ever blessing, ever blest,
well-spring of the joy of living,
ocean-depth of happy rest!

Thou our Father, Christ our Brother:
all who live in love are thine;
teach us how to love each other,
lift us to the joy divine.

Now thank we all our God (vs. 1–2)

Now thank we all our God, with heart, and hands, and voices,
who wondrous things hath done, in whom his world rejoices;
who from our mother's arms hath blessed us on our way
with countless gifts of love, and still is ours today.

O may this bounteous God through all our life be near us!
with ever-joyful hearts and blessed peace to cheer us;
and keep us in his grace, and guide us when perplexed,
and free us from all ills in this world and the next.

The spacious firmament

The spacious firmament on high,
with all the blue ethereal sky,
and spangled heavens, a shining frame,
their great Original proclaim.
The unwearied sun from day to day
does his Creator's power display;
and publishes to every land
the work of an almighty hand.

Soon as the evening shades prevail,
the moon takes up the wondrous tale,
and nightly to the listening earth
repeats the story of her birth:
whilst all the stars that round her burn,
and all the planets in their turn,
confirm the tidings, as they roll
and spread the truth from pole to pole.

What though in solemn silence all
move round the dark terrestrial ball?
What though no real voice nor sound
amid their radiant orbs be found?
In reason's ear they all rejoice,
and utter forth a glorious voice;
for ever singing as they shine,
"The hand that made us is divine."

Take my life

Take my life and let it be consecrated, Lord, to thee;
take my moments and my days, let them flow in ceaseless praise.
Take my hands, and let them move at the impulse of thy love;
take my heart, it is thine own; it shall be thy royal throne.

Take my voice, and let me sing always, only, for my King;
take my intellect, and use every power as thou shalt choose.
Take my will, and make it thine; it shall be no longer mine.
Take myself, and I will be ever, only, all for thee.

Prayers and Quotations

Guide us waking, O Lord, and guard us sleeping; that awake
we may watch with Christ, and asleep we may rest in peace.
(Book of Common Prayer, p. 135)

Do all the good you can,
By all the means you can,
In all the ways you can,
In all the places you can,
At all the times you can,
To all the people you can,
As long as ever you can. *(John Wesley)*[6]

A Prayer Attributed to St. Francis

Lord, make us instruments of your peace. Where there is hatred, let us
sow love; where there is injury, pardon; where there is discord, union;
where there is doubt, faith; where there is despair, hope; where there
is darkness, light; where there is sadness, joy. Grant that we may not
so much seek to be consoled as to console; to be understood as to
understand; to be loved as to love. For it is in giving that we receive;
it is in pardoning that we are pardoned; and it is in dying that we are
born to eternal life. Amen. *(Book of Common Prayer, p. 833)*

[A]ll shall be well and all shall be well and all manner of thing shall be
well. *(Julian of Norwich)*[7]

For the Care of Children

Almighty God, heavenly Father, you have blessed us with the joy and care of children: Give us calm strength and patient wisdom as we bring them up, that we may teach them to love whatever is just and true and good, following the example of our Savior Jesus Christ. Amen. *(Book of Common Prayer, p. 829)*

For Education

Almighty God, the fountain of all wisdom: Enlighten by your Holy Spirit those who teach and those who learn, that, rejoicing in the knowledge of your truth, they may worship you and serve you from generation to generation; through Jesus Christ our Lord, who lives and reigns with you and the Holy Spirit, one God, for ever and ever. Amen. *(Book of Common Prayer, p. 261)*

Having an epiphany is never planned. It is always a surprise. It always gives us just a little glimmer, opens a tiny window, into the mystery that is the nature of God. It is never hokey or romantic, but it can be shocking or disturbing.

The Season of Epiphany is a wondrous time to take in the miracle of God's creation. In the midst of the "bleak midwinter" when the sky is dark gray, the trees bare and brittle, and the ground is hard and cold, take time to ponder the common, everyday miracles around you. *(Elizabeth Kaeton, The Season of Epiphanies)*

Independence Day Collect

Lord God Almighty, in whose Name the founders of this country won liberty for themselves and for us, and lit the torch of freedom for nations then unborn: Grant that we and all the people of this land may have grace to maintain our liberties in righteousness and peace; through Jesus Christ our Lord, who lives and reigns with you and the Holy Spirit, one God, for ever and ever. Amen. *(Book of Common Prayer, p. 242)*

Life Blessing

Beloveds, the blessing of God is upon us
and God's mercy is over all that constitutes our lives.
All that we have been, are now, and will yet be
—that which seems light and that which seems dark—
all is held in God's wisdom and love.
We are called to embrace the life
which has been entrusted to us
and which we share with all that is,
visible and invisible.
May we remember all our beginnings
and know ourselves in the Love
that makes and keeps us one:
One God, in Three Persons,
now and always.
Amen.
(Ann Prentice, Order of Saint Helena)

For the Mission of the Church

> Everliving God, whose will it is that all should come to you through
> your Son Jesus Christ: Inspire our witness to him, that all may know
> the power of his forgiveness and the hope of his resurrection; who
> lives and reigns with you and the Holy Spirit, one God, now and for
> ever. Amen. *(Book of Common Prayer, pp. 816–817)*

Now let me say that the next thing we must be concerned about if
we are to have peace on earth and good will toward men is the non-
violent affirmation of the sacredness of all human life. Every man is
somebody because he is a child of God. *(Martin Luther King Jr.)*[8]

Christ has no body but yours,
No hands, no feet on earth but yours,
Yours are the eyes through which he looks
Compassion on this world,
Yours are the feet with which he walks to do good,
Yours are the hands, with which he blesses all the world.
Yours are the hands, yours are the feet,
Yours are the eyes, you are his body.
Christ has no body now but yours,
No hands, no feet on earth but yours,
Yours are the eyes through which he looks
Compassion on this world.
Christ has no body now on earth but yours. *(Teresa of Avila)*[9]

The Song of Simeon

> Lord, now lettest thou thy servant depart in peace,
> according to thy word;
> For mine eyes have seen thy salvation,
> which thou has prepared before the face of all people,
> To be a light to lighten the Gentiles,
> and to be the glory of thy people Israel. *(Book of Common Prayer, p. 66)*

Something in your life shows God at work. The primary work of God on earth is bringing good out of evil. You miss the mark if you see evil and conclude that there is no God. Look straight at the evil, and then look right next to it: what is God bringing about? What can happen in the ashes of it? *(Barbara Cawthorne Crafton, From the Geranium Farm)*

A SCRAPBOOK TIMELINE

Greek and Roman times The word "album" dates from a time when edicts and other announcements were written on stone or metal or wood (but white) tablets.

Medieval times Scribes sometimes extend their work to produce emblem books, which are bound pages of drawings with accompanying interpretations of allegorical meaning.

1550 Giorgio Vasari (1511–1574) writes about hundreds of artists in his *Lives of the Most Eminent Italian Architects, Painters, and Sculptors*. Vasari advocates keeping works of art in albums, and his method influences the beginnings of museums and libraries all over the world.

1600 From this century dates the development of commonplace books, in which "good sayings and notable observations" are recorded.

1600–1601 In this year, Shakespeare directs Hamlet to write into his tables or his commonplace book. "Smile and smile and be a villain," Hamlet says as he records notes to himself.

1650   The popularity of the *Kunstkammer* among the wealthy reaches a decided peak. This, the cabinet of curiosities, is a room or chest where objects such as stuffed monkeys, botanicals, statuary, jewelry and diverse exotica can be kept. The album finds a home, then, within the *Kunstkammer* or is itself the poor man's cabinet of curiosities.

1600–1700   This period also witnesses the development of the use of albums to keep prints and drawings. Following Vasari's advice, "serious amateurs, including Samuel Pepys, preserved most of their prints in this way. Such volumes constituted the backbone of every collection or 'cabinet' formed during that period. These albums are rare in the United States but much more common in Europe, where the tradition of making them continued until the 20th century. A large proportion of the 20 million prints in the Bibliothèque Nationale are still in such volumes."*

1706   The use of a commonplace book becomes even more popular after John Locke publishes his *New Method of Making Common-Place Books*, in which he instructs others on how best to preserve proverbs, maxims, ideas, references, meditations, self-cultivation and speeches.

1769   William Granger publishes a history of England in which he introduces extra prints illustrative of its text. In a later edition, he extends this idea by including blank pages on which could be pasted whatever appropriate illustration a purchaser might

*See http://www.well.com/user/bronxbob/resume/54_7-93.html—*Scrapbooks, the Smiling Villains* by Robert DeCandido

choose. Once conceived, a grangerized book comes to mean a sort of hybrid in which pages are changed, sometimes disbound and rebound, and/or altered by the addition of illustrations, letters, autographs or other placements. These strange combinations of printed book and scrapbook, also known as extra-illustrated books, reach the zenith of their popularity in the 19th century.

1792   Color printing revolutionizes contact with the visual world. The late 1790s see the beginning of this technology, though not yet frequently used across Europe.

1799   Scraps (die-cut glossy printed paper images) appear. Developed in Germany, these *glandzbilder*, chromos or scraps are the leftovers of a printing job and sometimes are recycled to the bakers' trade for wrapping special breads. Collectors become interested in preserving them in scrapbooks or, as one would say in Danish, *glansbillede* albums. These albums would become most popular in the late 19th century, but their appearance as early as 1799 is met with much excitement.

1800–1900   The early 19th century is the heyday of the friendship album, a book in which people keep the autographs, poetry, prose and wishes of their friends. Often passed between old and new acquaintances, these books increasingly are considered a feminine form of keeping memories.

1800–1900   Other printing inventions and improvements in engraving, letterpress and lithography result in more collectible paper. Ephemera, throwaway printed paper artifacts, become a part of everyday life.

1819   The publication of *The Complete Course of Lithography* by
Senefelder popularizes chromolithography, extending the reach
of chromos to England and the Americas.

1820   Publisher John Taylor makes available *A Pocket Common Place
with Locke Index*, thus furthering the reach of John Locke and
the tradition of the commonplace book.

1825   By this date, the term scrapbook is common enough that a
serial called *The Scrapbook* is issued, defining the hobby as the
keeping of a blank book in which pictures, newspaper cuttings
and the like are pasted for preservation. Scrapbooks marketed
widely throughout the 19th century include *Shipment's
Common Sense Binder*, *The Alexander Graham Bell Scrapbook*
and *The Ideal Patented Scrapbook*, among others.

1837   Louis-Jacques Daguerre invents the daguerreotype, the first
practical process of photography. His invention (with help
from Joseph Nicéphore Niepce and Claude Félix Abel Niepce
de Saint-Victor) will be followed quickly by improvements from
many others. Collectively, these inventors provide a new item to
include in scrapbooks—photographs—and change forever the
way we remember our own lives.

1839   Daguerreotype and Calotype processes are made public; hence
the "birth of photography" often is given as 1839.

1839   Members of the American Anti-Slavery Society begin clipping
from the Southern press, accumulating evidence of the cruelty
of slavery in the words of the slaveholders. The anti-slavery

forces amass these clippings in a scrapbook, which they publish as *American Slavery As It Is: Testimony of a Thousand Witnesses*. In the next decade, this book would be almost as important as Stowe's *Uncle Tom's Cabin* in advocating an end to slavery.

1844   William Henry Fox Talbot publishes the first book with photographs, *The Pencil of Nature*. Talbot is important for many reasons, but especially in terms of scrapbook history, for his invention of a process that includes negatives, and thus multiple prints of photographs, and for his work about producing photographs on paper.

1847   Louis Désiré Blanquard-Evard improves on Talbot's Calotype process and sets up a photographic printing establishment.

1850   Blanquard-Evard introduces albumen printing paper and assembles albums of photographs for customers.

1850   Mathew Brady issues the *Gallery of Illustrious Americans*, an album of 12 lithographic portraits from photographs. Available on a subscription basis, the portraits might be seen as a forerunner to many "false" scrapbooks that will be popular throughout the 19th and 20th centuries. With such publications, the images of politicians and other stars come into the homes of many Americans.

1850–1860   Hippolyte Bayard, Eugene Appert, Henry Peach Robinson, Oscar Rejlander and others experiment with photomontage. Amateur photographers will use similar techniques, as well, to add to albums and scrapbooks.

1852   Talbot patents a prototype of photo-engraving, a precursor to the development in the 1880s of the more successful halftone plates.

1855   Alphonse Poitevin, a French chemist, discovers two methods for printing with potassium bichromate; these methods develop into photolithography and carbon printing.

1857   *Carte-de-visite* photographs arrive in the U.S., producing a craze similar to one begun with their introduction in Europe (1854). *Carte-de-visite* albums contain a pocket for the insertion of photographs.

1860   The first advertisement in the national press for photographic albums is printed in *Harpers Weekly 4., no. 208* (December 22, 1860): 815.

1872   Mark Twain markets his patented scrapbook. Twain would make $50,000 from these scrapbooks, described as self-pasting and available though Daniel Slote and Company. "Use but little moisture and only on the gummed lines. Press the scrap on without wetting it." Twain holds patents in England, France and the U.S. and works hard to improve his self-pasting methods.

1880   The Eastman Dry Plate Company is founded.

1880   Stephen Horgan's "A Scene in Shantytown" is printed in "halftone" in the *New York Daily Graphic*. Thus begins an era where people may clip photographs as well as the written word from the newspaper and other publications.

1880   E. W. Gurley publishes *Scrap-books and How to Make Them*, a book that notes the foolishness of letting a good article go to waste. "Scrapbooks are necessary. The American public now has 8,000 newspapers, as opposed to 2 in the times of Franklin. [Too] Gossipy reading can be cured if we read for a purpose, look for something, and keep it when found . . . in the pages of a good scrapbook."

1881   Frederick E. Ives invents the photoengraving process.

1886   Frederick E. Ives further develops the halftone engraving process such that it becomes possible to reproduce photo-graphic images in the same operation as printed text.

1888   Eastman markets the Kodak camera and roll film.

1897   The *New Orleans Times Picayune* promotes the scrapbook in a society column, noting that a memory book is "an interesting tablet for the girl of the present time to keep. . . . One New Orleans girl who is famous for her beauty and favoritism in the social world . . . has a record of her social triumphs perpetuated in her memory book, as well as several very charming sketches of herself. . . ."

1898   W.E.B. Dubois publishes his *The Philadelphia Negro; a Social Study*. In the preface, he acknowledges his debt to William Dorsey and his collection of scrapbooks. In the late 19th and early 20th centuries, Dorsey creates some 300 scrapbooks, cutting from the press to accumulate a vast resource on the lives of African-Americans.

1900   The first mass-marketed camera, The Brownie, appears.

1900–1930   Publishers such as Dodd, Mead; Paul Elder; Lippincott; and others tap into the market for scrapbooks by publishing illustrated and annotated books for school children, high school and college women, and new mothers. Also published are bride books and First Communion books. Organizations wishing to commemorate the passing of their members even have bound books for death notices.

1905–1915   The postcard fad adds another dimension to collecting. Some albums and scrapbooks are marketed particularly for these cards.

1906   Panchromatic plates are marketed by Wratten & Wainright. Off-set lithography is invented.

1911–1912   Picasso and Braque, followed by many others such as Juan Gris and Joseph Cornell, experiment with collage. Of revolutionary importance in modern art, collage was the "high" art of something many scrapbook makers would recognize as their own technique of cutting and pasting.

1930   The photo album, first created in the 19th century, becomes the most common form of scrapbook in the 20th century.

1948   The Billy Rose Theatre Collection of New York Public Library is given a donation of some 300 scrapbooks filled by one man and his staff. The collection is received with the stipulation that approximately 18 boxes of ephemera would be added to new scrapbooks.

1950   The Xerox copying machine is introduced.

1963   The Kodak 156 Instamatic cartridge camera is introduced.

1970   T. Harry Williams publishes his biography of Huey Long. Like other historians, Williams relies often on the scrapbooks of news clippings, thus offering a Louisiana example of how such albums are cited by scholars.

1980   Mormon Marielen W. Christensen generates intense interest when she displays her memory albums, featuring scrapbook pages inserted into plastic page protectors inside three-ring binders, at the World Conference on Records in Salt Lake City, Utah. She and her husband Anthony open a memory-book supply store and mail-order company a year later.

1987   Creative Memories, a direct sales company, begins marketing scrapbooks, fueling a new craze for this form of memory keeping.

For a bibliography on scrapbooks see http://www.tulane.edu/~wclib/susan.html—*Scrapbooks and Albums, Theories and Practice: An Annotated Bibliography* by Danielle Bias, Rebecca Black, and Susan Tucker

Timeline created by Susan Tucker, curator of books and records at the Newcomb College Center for Research on Women at Tulane University, New Orleans, and edited for this publication by Sharon Sheridan. Reprinted with permission from Susan Tucker.

RESOURCES

*H*ere's a sampling of resources for more information on scrapbooking and creating faith albums.

Creating Keepsakes. Founded in 1996, *Creating Keepsakes* began as a bimonthly magazine that now publishes thirteen times a year. The company also offers Creating Keepsakes University, scrapbook conventions and a website featuring products and books for sale, contests, album-making tips, a newsletter and a message board. *Creating Keepsakes Magazine*, 14850 Pony Express Road, Bluffdale, UT; 800-984-2070; website www.creatingkeepsakes.com.

Creative Memories. A direct-sales company founded by Rhonda Anderson and Cheryl Lightle, Creative Memories sells albums and album-making products and guides through independent sales consultants who demonstrate products and teach album-making techniques, often through classes in scrappers' homes. They can provide classes and instruction specifically on "faithbooking," along with resources such as a biblical concordance. Creative Memories also sells *Lasting Moments* magazine. Creative Memories, P.O. Box 1839, 3001 Clearwater Road, St. Cloud, MN 56302-1839; 800-468-9335 (800-341-5275 to locate a consultant); website www.creativememories.com. Magazine subscriptions: Creative Memories, *Lasting Moments*, P.O. Box 37160, Boone, IA 50037-0160; 866-308-4126; or visit the website.

Keeping Memories Alive. Founded by Marielen and Anthony Christensen, Keeping Memories Alive sells scrapbooks and album-making products and guides online, wholesale, via mail orders and through authorized retailers. KMA offers classes at its retail site in Spanish Fork, Utah. Keeping Memories Alive, 260 N. Main, Spanish Fork, UT 84660; 800-419-4949; e-mail kma@scrapbooks.com; website www.scrapbooks.com.

Memory Makers, The Scrapbook Club. F+W Publications publishes *Memory Makers Magazine* and operates a book club for scrapbookers. Magazine subscriptions: *Memory Makers*, P.O. Box 420235, Palm Cost, FL 32142; 800-366-6465; website www.memorymakersmagazine.com. Club subscriptions: Member Service Department, The ScrapBook Club, 580 S. Research Place, Central Islip, NY 11722-4416; 386-246-3404; website www.thescrapbookclubonline.com.

Mrs. Grossman's. Founded by Andrea Grossman, this company sells a wide variety of decorative stickers through retailers and via its website, which also features sticker clubs for kids and adults, sticker ideas and the company mission statement, which has a strong faith component. MGPC, P.O. Box 4467, Petaluma, CA 94955; 800-429-4549 or 707-763-1700; e-mail mgpc2@mgpc.net; website www.mrsgrossmans.com.

Praisebooking.com. This Internet site, which describes itself as "an online forum for Christian scrapbooking," includes a gallery of page layouts by members. Website www.praisebooking.com.

Reminders of Faith. Reminders of Faith provides information and inspiration on telling stories of God's faithfulness through scrapbooking. It sells scrapbooks and album-making products and guides; provides referrals to retailers, consultants, scrapbook retreats and related websites; sponsors contests; and more. Reminders of Faith, 518 Overhead Drive, Moon Township, PA 15108; 800-699-4964; website www.remindersoffaith.com.

Scrapbooks etc. Better Homes and Gardens *Scrapbooks etc.* magazine publishes eight issues a year. Website features include information on scrapbook supplies and techniques, a store locator, videos, an online gallery of scrapbook pages and blogs of scrappers. *Scrapbooks etc.*, 1716 Locust Street-LN 414, Des Moines, IA 50309-3023; 800-688-6611; website www.bhgscrapbooksetc.com.

StoryTellers. StoryTellers sells exclusive products based around monthly themes. The online StoryTellers Club offers features such as galleries of page layouts, discussions, contests and weekly challenges, products for sale and information on digital scrapping. StoryTellers, P.O. Box 1201, Cedar City, UT 84721; 877-727-2701; e-mail CustomerService@StoryTellersClub.com or Sales@StoryTellersClub.com; website www.storytellersclub.com.

BOOKS

Our Family Scrapbooks. By Lisa Bearnson and Becky Higgins, Primedia, Inc., 2005.

Passing on Your Legacy of Love: Scrapbooking with a Purpose. By Marci Whitford, Reminders of Faith, Inc., 2004.

Scrapbooking Your Spiritual Journey: Inspiring You to Tell the Stories of God's Faithfulness to Future Generations. By Sandra L. Joseph, Reminders of Faith, Inc., 2003.

The Scrapbook in American Life. Edited by Susan Tucker, Katherine Ott and Patricia P. Buckler, Temple University Press, 2006.

NOTES

1. *The Oxford Dictionary of Quotations, Third Edition* (New York: Oxford University Press, 1980), 118.

2. *Book of Occasional Services* (New York: The Church Pension Fund, 2004), 163.

3. *The Oxford Dictionary of Quotations, Third Edition*, 216.

4. Bob Williams, "Shanghai cathedral photos, blueprints sought to aid restoration; Anglicans asked to consult family albums, church archives," Episcopal News Service (November 14, 2005).

5. *The Oxford Dictionary of Quotations, Third Edition*, 150.

6. From "Rule of Conduct" in *The Oxford Dictionary of Quotations, Third Edition*, 568.

7. From "Revelations of Divine Love" in *The Oxford Dictionary of Quotations, Third Edition*, 286.

8. From "A Christmas Sermon on Peace" (1967) in James M. Washington, ed., *A Testament of Hope: The Essential Writings and Speeches of Martin Luther King, Jr.* (San Francisco: HarperSanFrancisco, 1990), 255.

9. From untitled poem, quoted in http://www.worldconcern.org/NETCOMMUNITY/Page.aspx?&pid=417&srcid=946, accessed March 30, 2007.